BV 3790 .B76 1945 c.1
Bryan, Dawson Charles, 1900-
A workable plan of evangelism.

A Workable Plan of Evangelism

DAWSON C. BRYAN

They that be wise shall shine as the brightness of the firmament; and they that turn many to righteousness as the stars for ever and ever.—DANIEL 12:3

Abingdon - Cokesbury Press

NEW YORK • NASHVILLE

A WORKABLE PLAN OF EVANGELISM

COPYRIGHT, MCMXLV
By WHITMORE & STONE

All rights in this book are reserved. No part of the text may be reproduced in any form without written permission of the publishers, except brief quotations used in connection with reviews in magazines or newspapers.

Wartime Books

Wartime shortage of pulp, manpower, and transportation has produced a severe shortage of paper. In compliance with orders of the War Production Board, wartime books are printed on lighter-weight paper. This reduces thickness and weight. New books have more words to the page and smaller margins. This reduces the number of pages without reducing reading content.

Thinner books save paper, critical copper, and other metals. They help also to avoid wartime increases in book prices. Wartime books appear to be smaller, but their content has not been cut. They are complete. The only change is in appearance.

Printed in the United States of America

To
MY DAUGHTER MARGIE
*Who Naturally and Normally Has Always
Known the Love of the Heavenly Father*

PREFACE

THE CHRISTIAN CHURCH BEGAN AND CONTINUES ITS growth in a very simple but profound fashion—witness bearing. It has been said that when a person is truly converted he passes his conversion on to others. John records that when Andrew confessed Jesus, immediately he found his brother Peter and brought him to the Master. Philip sought out Nathanael, and as the Word was shared the message has come down through the generations. So to his sincere and loyal followers of the present hour God gives the grace to follow in this train.

Every church can be an evangelistic church. Every church can win more converts than has been its custom. Laymen can know the joy of winning others to the faith. Christ's method of securing followers has a modern application which can bring a great revival of religion. This book might well be entitled "Jesus' Method of Evangelism," for he and the apostles used it extensively. Here are methods to match our times, ways in which every church can project its life into the community and expect favorable decisions.

Part I outlines the plan for the study of the pastor and also for profit to any interested layman. Part II gives the instruction talks which the pastor uses in training his laymen to become effective visitors.

Most of the program presented is not mine. It is not novel. It originated with Jesus. It has been worked out through years of experience by many pastors and churches. It is presented in this form because it is practical and adaptable to any and every church.

I am indebted to many persons, ministers and laymen, and particularly to Dr. Guy H. Black, who first introduced me to the methods of visitation evangelism, and who probably more than any other person has contributed to their effectiveness. I wish to express appreciation to my wife, to the staff of St. Paul's Church, to my secretary, Mrs. Amanda Gardiner, and to the men of the "Fishermen's Club" of St. Paul's Church, who through the years have been so faithful and effective as Christ's ambassadors.

Charles Heimsath has written, "Into the dark stream of our common life has flowed a fresh current of a faith that is irresistible." I believe that to be true. It is the purpose of this book that we may be so captured by that fresh current of evangelical faith that we shall transmit it splendidly and radiantly to others.

DAWSON C. BRYAN

St. Paul's Methodist Church
Houston, Texas

CONTENTS

PART I

THE PLAN OF VISITATION EVANGELISM

I. ORGANIZING THE CHURCH FOR EVANGELISM 11
II. FINDING THE PROSPECTS 24
    How to find and prepare lists of prospective members
III. SECURING THE VISITORS 42
    How to choose and select suitable and effective personal workers
IV. USING TRAINED VISITORS 53
    Various methods and occasions for using trained workers in personal visitation
V. TRAINING THE VISITORS 76
    How to train visitors to do effective personal work
VI. ASSIMILATING NEW MEMBERS 87
    How to integrate new members into church life

PART II

THE INSTRUCTION OF THE VISITORS

INTRODUCTION TO PART II 100
VII. SECURING THE DECISION 102
VIII. EFFICIENT VISITING 116
IX. DIFFICULT CASES 131

A WORKABLE PLAN OF EVANGELISM

X. FAMILY VISITING AND THE CONTINUATION
   PROGRAM 144

APPENDIX: AN OUTLINE FOR A VISITATION PROGRAM...... 159

SAMPLES OF PRINTED FORMS

A. Family Survey Card 27
B. Roll Call Card 33
C. Prospect and Assignment Card........................... 39
D. Visitor's Agreement Card 47
E. New Member and Sponsor Record..................... 95
F. Record of Decision Card..................................... 115
G. Nine Points of Efficient Visiting......................... 117
H. Summary of Reports of Visitation 118

PART I: THE PLAN OF VISITATION EVANGELISM

CHAPTER I

Organizing the Church for Evangelism

NEVER IN THE HISTORY OF CHRISTENDOM HAS THERE been a greater need for a spiritual awakening than today. Never has there been so imperative a demand for Christian men and for Christian solutions in personal and social problems. And never in the Christian centuries has there been a more effective means for the revival of men than the method of lay evangelism which is now being used in American Protestantism.

Once in a long time a powerful force becomes available while at the same moment some method is found to transform that power into useful service. At the turn of this twentieth century there was such a coincidence. Oil in substantial quantities was discovered. At just about the same time the internal combustion engine, which is the powerhouse of the automobile and airplane was invented. Either oil or engines without the other would have been practically useless. Many a farmer was pestered with the sticky black substance that seeped into his pond, spoiling the water for his stock. When automobiles needed that oily substance for power, then those farmers became wealthy, and the era of oil-driven motors began.

The power of God is the supreme necessity in the lives of men. It is as necessary as oil for motors. And there have been times when men have invented methods of making that power available to mankind, with astonishing results. One such method has been revival services or, as they have been called, "protracted meetings," or "special meetings." There have been periods when this has been the primary way by which people have been won into the kingdom. Again there have been other times when its usefulness has faded. We seem to be in one of those depression periods when for many churches revivals do not secure the results which once attended them.

But God does not leave himself without witness. There is a method at hand that is being used by many churches and many pastors. It has within it the means of transmitting God's power for the evangelization of America. Again the strange coincidence: power and a method of using it!

The winds of the Spirit

For a moment let us change our figure to a more scriptural one. The winds of the Spirit are blowing again across our land. They are bringing from the high mountains of God a reviving and refreshing coolness to the arid desert of modern life. These winds of the Spirit also have power to regenerate the lives of men, to tune in again the music and the wonder of Christian civilization and brotherhood.

A few years ago two brothers found that they were too poor to have the batteries for the radio in their farm home charged as often as they ran down. Necessity being the mother of invention, they devised the little propeller seen spinning rapidly at so many farm homes today. These propellers turn with the slightest breeze and operate little generators which charge the batteries of radios to bring in again contacts with the wide world. The little invention of these two youths made it possible to harness the winds to recharge batteries not only for radios but in many cases for lights and power.

In recent years there have been spiritually sensitive men who, knowing that God does not leave himself without witness, and in an urgency born of great necessity, have discovered a method by which the winds of the Spirit may be transmitted to men for their regeneration.

God is always ready for a revival of religion. The hindrances to spiritual awakening are with men, either in the lack of passion for souls or because they have no adequate method of harnessing the winds of the Spirit. Often the Godly breeze of gentle stillness is enough, if properly captured and used, to revive and quicken a trembling soul. Or again there comes the mighty rushing wind that sweeps multitudes into the Kingdom. There must be both the intense desire to see people won to Christ and a practical method by which they can be reached for a decision.

There are some ministers who do not have this earnest and compelling desire to seek people for the Christian life. They have seen the methods which they have used, and which once had their day of effectiveness, fade into the shadows. Some still go through the motions of revival services, hardly expecting any decisions, for they know that the non-church people whom they would reach do not attend their services.

A WORKABLE PLAN OF EVANGELISM

In the past when revival services were announced the church would be filled, often crowded. Everybody would come. There were those who were saints and many who admitted they were sinners. During the services the saints were revived and many of the sinners were converted.

Today when revival services are announced, who are in attendance? In all too many churches the congregation is made up almost entirely of church members. There are the saints, or those who think they are saints. The sinners are conspicuous by their absence. The people whom the church would reach for Christ are not present.

Recently I attended a revival meeting. At the close of a good sermon the preacher gave the invitation, and between stanzas of the hymn he repeated the call with great fervency. Then, as no one responded, he asked the Christians to raise their hands. It appeared that every hand was raised. Then he requested those who were not members of any church anywhere to raise their hands. One man timidly ventured to put his hand up.

This experience is not an isolated one. While there are some churches and some denominations where results are being secured in assembled congregations, most churches either cannot or do not find unconverted people attending special services. Most churches need to face the fact that the people whom they wish to reach are outside the church services. Jesus went where the people were, and Paul said, "I am become all things to all men, that I may by all means save some." Therefore we must adopt methods which seek out and find these who need God most. If they will not attend church, we must take the gospel message to them.

Many of our ministers have become discouraged and frustrated because the means once used is seldom effective today. Some preachers are affected by the resulting inferiority complex, often even questioning their call to the ministry. Others excuse themselves by saying that the regular church members need reviving and that professions of faith are not made as once they were.

In the Methodist Church, which is not far different from most others, in 1943 out of 20,993 active pastors there were 2,983 who did not have a single new member added to the church on profession of faith. In addition, 10,236 received between one and twelve on profession of faith. Not having a method which is productive of results, ministers and congregations find the evangelistic ardor cooling, and in an attitude of self-protection they turn their efforts to other endeavors.

A new encouragement

But this is not a time for discouragement in evangelism. Quite the contrary. For those who have eyes to see and ears to hear, God has provided a means which may prove not only as effective as methods of old, but even far more effective. No man dare say that the time will never return when people may be won to Christ again in mass meetings. That day may be nearer than many people think. In fact some churches are quite successful with it now. If and when mass evangelism is effective, let us use it for every spiritual value it may have. But in the meantime there is at hand the possibility of the greatest revival of religion America has ever seen.

In the revivals men were brought to the altar of the church, where they received the empowering Spirit of God. In visitation evangelism the church is taken into the homes of the people, where an altar of dedication is erected, and where, in the sanctity of the family, they receive the transforming Spirit of God.

Family visitation evangelism is a new method, but it is not a new invention. It is the rediscovery of a procedure over nineteen hundred years old. It is an adaptation of the way instituted by Jesus for the conversion of men. It is the approach he himself used, the method in which he trained his followers.

Jesus' use of trained laymen

This program of visitation evangelism follows the program originated by Jesus. In the same spirit of prayer as when he chose the twelve, Jesus selected seventy other disciples and sent them out two by two as his official representatives.

In Luke 10:2 we find those oft-repeated words, "The harvest truly is great, but the laborers are few: pray ye therefore the Lord of the harvest, that he would send forth laborers into his harvest." In this passage Jesus prayerfully selects these seventy lay followers to whom he gives careful instructions. They are to go as his ambassadors, two by two. He describes in detail what they are to expect and how to approach the people whom they are to win to the Kingdom. It is most rewarding for a minister or layman to study and ponder this most unusual proceeding. For no other religious leader, anywhere in the world, prior to Jesus, ever used a group of lay people to proclaim his coming and enlist followers.

This group of seventy carefully chosen disciples stand before Jesus. He gives them instructions. He first makes their assignments, dividing the territory geographically. They are to go in pairs, but no two teams are to go to the same place. He tells them what to expect, how to make their approach, what to say, how to win people to the new discipleship, how to inform them of the coming Master, what will happen when rejections come, and that when disappointments are met, they are not to be discouraged. Then he sends them out, "two by two before his face into every city and place, whither he himself would come."

The miracle occurs! Led by the Spirit of God they do as the Master has instructed them, and when they return, their hearts are filled with joy. Far more happened than they had ever expected. The spirits of evil had been dispersed, people had responded, disciples had been won, they had "cleared a free way for the feet of God," and rejoicing they returned to report to Jesus.

Jesus used this method himself

Jesus not only trained his disciples in personal evangelism but used this method himself. Undoubtedly many people came to hear Christ preach, and many who heard him followed him. But the names of those we know, those found in the gospel records, almost without exception were won by Christ in personal interviews. He chose his own disciples personally. In the Gospel of John are recorded fourteen personal interviews Jesus had with others. One night he discussed spiritual rebirth with Nicodemus. In a personal interview with the woman at the well he spoke redeeming words that changed her life. She immediately went to tell those in her city. And through his conversation with her unnumbered people across the centuries have worshiped God in spirit and in truth. In the home of Zacchaeus the interview led to the transformation not only of Zacchaeus but also of his entire household.

Jesus won Andrew. Andrew introduced Peter, his brother, to Christ. Philip met Jesus and ran to find Nathanael to tell him about the Messiah. Thus the age-long process began—and continues even now, as people witness in person for Christ.

A pattern for today

So Jesus set the pattern for modern visitation evangelism. Jesus designed and projected a method nineteen hundred years ago which produces the same amazing results today. With fidelity to the first visitation evangelistic program instituted by Jesus, a pastor designs and projects a similar enterprise in a modern American community.

The program of personal home evangelism follows the pattern of Jesus in almost every detail. Observe the amazing similarity. The pastor prayerfully and diligently chooses laymen who are to be sent out. They are also paired, two by two. They are assigned to prospects previously selected and geographically grouped. They meet together for instructions, the pastor indicating what they shall find, the difficulties they shall meet, those who shall respond, and the best means of winning them. He tells them of the ones who will reject the claims of Christ and the church. He cautions them against discouragement. Most amazing of all, there is the return of these visitors with their reports of success for the Kingdom and the great joy like the rejoicing of the seventy of old, or like the angels who are overjoyed when sinners repent and turn to God.

The parallel is perfect. Jesus' method in evangelism is being reborn in our generation. And where pastors and laymen use it, they see literally thousands upon thousands of new converts, as well as people renewing their loyalty as active members.

For large and small churches

Some minister objects, "This plan may do well enough in a large church where there are enough people to select competent workers and where there is a secretary to do the clerical work, but it is impractical in a small church."

Quite the contrary. Some of the most remarkable evangelistic visitation programs have been conducted in small churches and in sparse communities. A secretary is not necessary. In a small church the clerical work is limited. Most pastors take care of it themselves or appoint a layman to do so. This plan is simple enough for a church of fifty members with perhaps only two visitors, and it is complete enough for a church of several thousand members with perhaps a hundred visitors. It secures decisions in crowded cities, in quiet towns, and in the open country. Jesus' method of personal approach, like the love of God, reads "whosoever will." There are no limitations, except those we throw around it.

In the Riverside Church in San Antonio with forty-seven members and four visitors, eighteen persons united with the church on Membership Sunday, ten of those coming on profession of faith. Here was a small church that had an increase of 38 per cent in membership in four nights of visiting.

A few days prior to a district-wide visitation campaign the pastor of a rural church of less than a hundred members said to his superintendent, "I can't participate. I've been able to secure only two visitors. It's hopeless, and I don't have much faith in this plan anyway. Just count our church out."

"Oh, no!" replied the superintendent. "You wouldn't want to do that. You agreed to participate. For the sake of the morale of the others, some of whom are also fainthearted, you can't withdraw. It would weaken the movement." So the pastor reluctantly went ahead. He was given the instructions, which each night he passed on to his two laymen. Before the end of the week both the pastor and the laymen were most enthusiastic. Scriptural joy came to them. New life entered that little congregation, for nineteen new members were added—more in that one week than in several years previously.

This method is beyond the experimental stage. It has proved its worth all across America for churches in every kind of situation. In one city a pastor began his pastorate with a few less than three hundred members. In one week of training conferences accompanied by visiting in the homes he trained a group of lay people, mostly young couples. These visitors met and called one evening each month. In the five years of that pastorate the membership increased to a net of over eight hundred. The church debt was paid, a new educational building was erected and nearly paid for, and the attendance at church services increased so much that each Sunday morning two identical church services were required. This method works whenever it is honestly tried.

A revival without preaching

A serious question is raised that this procedure secures decisions without the preaching which is so necesary to bring the people to a thorough understanding of the gospel which they are about to accept. It is estimated, however, that nineteen out of twenty persons called upon in visitation evangelism have attended some church or church school or both at some times in their lives. The claims of the Christian life are not unknown to them. Almost all of them have heard preaching, but they have not acted upon it.

Someone has said, "The worst man knows more good than the best man practices." While that isn't true, it contains enough truth to indicate that almost everyone who is a prospect for church membership knows enough about the Christian religion and the saving power of Christ to decide to become one of his followers, if he wants to do so.

Any person who wishes further light than the lay visitor can give him ought to be directed to have an interview with the pastor. Then the pastor will have plenty of opportunity to give specific help to the penitent seeker.

One of the finest developments to come out of the visitation evangelistic movement is that some ministers follow the period of visitation and the securing of decisions with a week or more of special worship services where the new members, as well as the old, may have their faith validated in the Word of God brought from the pulpit.

Skilled servants of Christ

If the war has taught us one thing it is the value of highly trained men. The war quickly became one of skill. The men and women in military service were disciplined in every sort of complicated technique in an incredibly short time. High proficiency was attained so quickly by eliminating all extraneous matter and insisting on superior quality.

Winning people to Christ is an enterprise of skill. While a person may be converted through a simple and sincere word or example, that is not enough if we are to win an entire nation to our Lord. A passion for souls is an essential, but such desire to win the victory is not sufficient. Shoddy presentation of the claims of Christ's kingdom, if not inexcusable, is certainly unnecessary.

Christ's method of securing followers by personal solicitation has a present-day application which can bring a great revival of religion. The plan is simple and may be taught by any pastor to the choice laymen of his congregation. It is specific and may be learned quickly in a few intensive nights of instruction and visiting. It meets the test of Christ by producing the fruits of new members for his church.

As the pastor sets about the plans in his own church he may be assured that his faith will be amply rewarded. He will be sustained by God, whose desire is that not one of these may be lost, and the limits of his endeavor will be dependent only upon the fidelity with which he and his people commit themselves to the program.

Arthur Schnabel, the interpreter of Beethoven, once remarked, "I only play music that is better than it can be played." That is the sort of music that the world needs to stir it—better music than can be played. But it needs artists who endeavor to play it to perfection. The music of God's love for the redemption of the world is greater than any of us can ever play, but we can give to it all the devotion of which we are capable. Through high motive and effective methods the pastor and his people may enter into the symphony of winning people to Christ and his eternal Kingdom.

CHAPTER II

Finding the Prospects

"THERE ARE NO UNCHURCHED PEOPLE IN MY COMMUNITY," explained one pastor. He was one of the amazingly large number of ministers in one seventh of all the churches in America who had not a single new member added to his church that year on profession of faith.

Shortly afterward a new preacher came to that little church. His predecessor neglected to advise him that there were no prospects for church membership, so the new minister made a community survey. The result was that he discovered 118 persons who were prospects for his own church alone. Some of these were members of his denomination elsewhere. The remainder made no Christian profession, but if they were to unite with any church it would be in his denomination. During that year he secured forty-three of these as new members for his church.

DISCOVERING THE HIDING PLACES

While Jesus commanded, "Go out into the highways and hedges, and compel them to come in," such an injunction is useless unless we know on what highway some churchless man is living or behind what hedge he is hiding.

There are people without Christ in every community. But who are they? Where do they live? What are their names and addresses?

FINDING THE PROSPECTS

"How can I find the people in my community who are prospective members for my church?" is the inquiry of many a pastor. To have the information that 48 per cent of America is unchurched means nothing, less than nothing. But to know that Mrs. Barclay Brown, who is a Baptist, has a husband who is not a Christian should point out to the Baptist minister that behind the front hedge at 1635 South Highway is a man who ought to be at the Lord's table in the Baptist church.

There are several methods by which a pastor may know exactly who the "Barclay Browns" in his community are and where they live.

1. An interdenominational community survey

In a certain community the ministers of the majority of the churches met and planned a community survey. They knew that the most thorough and accurate method of inquiry is a community survey in which every home in the entire community is visited. In such a survey the name and address of every person who has no local church home is written down on an appropriate survey card.

These ministers realized that this was a difficult undertaking, but they also knew that it yielded the maximum results. By it no single individual would be missed. They set up three committees. The first committee selected the specific areas for each church to canvass. Another committee was to tabulate the results. The third committee was to supply each pastor with the names and addresses of all persons showing preference for his denomination or local

A WORKABLE PLAN OF EVANGELISM

church. A family survey card (Form A, on the opposite page) was used.

Each pastor secured his own quota of canvassers. A training class was held for all the canvassers. Instruction was given as to how to make the proper approach, and how to get the *exact* information, particularly the location of church memberships and the church preferences of all nonchurch people. The survey was taken, and each pastor was given the cards listing his "prospects."

The result of the hard work was that every minister knew every "lost sheep of the house of Israel" who was his responsibility.

2. A community survey by a single church

A survey covering an entire community seems an impossibility for a single church, but "impossible" is a relative word. Charles F. Kettering says, "Incurable diseases are only those the doctors don't know how to cure." So an individual church can do the seemingly impossible and make a survey of its community.

The size of the community will determine the method used. In one of my early pastorates I personally visited every home in a town of 1,850 persons and then wrote down the church affiliations of all of them. I secured fifty-eight new members for my church that year even though I used the least effective method, for I secured almost all of those decisions myself. If I had known then the method of evangelism where the laymen do the calling, undoubtedly there would have been more new members

RELIGIOUS CENSUS

Family Name		Address		Telephone
Christian Names	Approx. Age	Members of what		If not a member of church what preference
		Church School	Church	
Father				
Mother				
Children				
Others living in home				

FORM A. FAMILY SURVEY CARD

A WORKABLE PLAN OF EVANGELISM

received. But at least that is an effective way to conduct a community survey—for the pastor to stop at the door of every home in his parish.

A few years ago we wanted to know all the Methodist prospects in our section of a large city of 500,000 population. An interdenominational survey was impractical at that time. It seemed as though the undertaking was totally impossible with the number of canvassers we could secure. Then one woman made a suggestion that was undoubtedly inspired: "We only want to find the Methodist prospects, don't we? Well, let's just ask at each home if there are any Methodists living there, or if there are non-church people whose preference is the Methodist church. If we find those of other denominations, let us wish them well in their churches, but we won't stop for any information about them."

And so we tried her system, finding it to work most effectively. The territory was divided among the canvassers, each worker being given a certain number of blocks. At each house the solicitor would ask if any Methodists lived there. If the answer was affirmative, then the information was written down on the family survey card. This was simple. But if the answer was negative, then the canvasser had to exert real care to find out about each non-church member to be certain whether he preferred the Methodist Church. If he had no preference, he was considered "our" prospect unless later visitation proved he was not. If any persons were not members of some other denomination, specific questions had to be asked so that no one might be passed by and lost. For here truly were those lost along the highway for whom our church alone was responsible. If no church preference was given, the final question was, "If you were to have a wedding or a funeral, what preacher would you call?" That always brought some church preference. The canvassers secured the written information about these whom they considered "Methodist" prospects.

By this method much time was saved because the canvassers passed by many of the homes with merely a friendly greeting. But the information we desired was secured. We obtained the names of those whom it was our responsibility to visit.

A community-wide survey is hard work. But it can be undertaken successfully, and its value is worth all the effort expended because it is the only known way to secure the information about *all* the prospective members, especially the non-Christians.

3. Church-school prospects

The most fertile field of prospects lies in the church school, its members and the parents of its children. These people are already interested in the church and Christ's Kingdom. They already have an attachment to a particular church. Persons enrolled in the church school who are not professed Christians or members of the local church are that church's primary responsibility. No other church will or can do anything about them. Likewise, if the parents unite with any church, it will naturally be the one where their children are attending the church school. If a child is attending church school and the parents are not members, they of all people are the most easily approached, and the most responsive.

A church school survey requires four weeks. On the first Sunday family survey cards (Form A, page 27) should be distributed in every department and class. Each pupil, teacher, and officer should fill out a card with complete information about all the members of his family. The absentees who attend during the following three Sundays should be requested to fill out cards. In the elementary departments the superintendents and teachers of the smaller children should fill in the information, securing it from the children, or by telephoning the parents.

Of course there will be duplicate cards because every member of each family in the church school will fill out a similar card. But it is better to get the information from mother, father, and two children of a family and then discard three cards than to miss a single person. It is easy to go over the final cards alphabetically and remove the duplicates. By one month's effort a complete prospect list of the church school can be compiled. Here will be gathered the most interested and available people to become new members of the congregation.

Upon completion of one church school survey the general superintendent exclaimed, "I had no idea so many prospects were connected with our school."

4. A roll call

The number of visitors at Sunday church services will depend upon the location of the church and its

FINDING THE PROSPECTS

constituents. A country church will have few visitors, most of whom will be well known to the church members. A downtown city church will have scores, possibly hundreds of visitors, most of whom will be strangers. But the average church will have more nonmembers in the pews than its members will suppose. The difficulty lies in discovering the presence of visitors and in getting their names and addresses.

One way to find the visitors at church services is to have a "Roll Call Sunday." This will not interfere with the regular church worship for the day. A Roll Call Sunday has a dual purpose, to note the presence of both members and visitors. A record of all the members of the church who are in attendance on the designated Sunday is secured. Visitors are asked also to record their presence. The Roll Call Card (Form B, page 33) gives the information showing whether the person is a church member, a visitor, a prospective member, or desires to become a member of the church immediately.

The ushers distribute the cards as persons enter the church. When the pastor is announcing the roll call, he simply states that all visitors are requested to join with the members in this record of attendance and that each person is asked to sign a card. At the same time he may extend a friendly greeting and welcome to the church and its services.

This method is particularly effective in churches located in urban areas or churches with large memberships. One downtown church secured the names of 128 visitors on a Roll Call Sunday. Eleven of these indicated their desire to unite with the church.

5. A register with a guardian

In a certain congregation there is a man who remembers names and faces. He stands at the entrance of the church, looking for strangers. He is not the back-slapping sort of person, but he is friendly and cordial. He sees a new face and introduces himself, graciously asking if the person is a visitor at the church. If so, he requests him to place his name in the visitors' register. In this particular church there are sometimes as many as forty or fifty visitors at a morning service, and the man naturally runs risks. Unknowingly he may inquire of some long-time member if he is attending his first service in the church. Then the sparks may fly!

In one large downtown church where unusual crowds attend services an elderly woman, a lifetime member and the church's most liberal supporter, who because of ill health could attend only occasionally, came late to church one morning. The young usher said, "I'm sorry, but the only remaining seats are up in the balcony."

"But young man, I don't want to climb the steps. Couldn't you put a chair for me by the chancel near the preacher?"

"I'm sorry," replied the young man, "but the fire regulations won't permit chairs in the aisles. And next Sunday every latecomer would want us to do the same for him."

"Young man, do you know who I am?" she asked.

"No," he replied quite candidly.

With a twinkle in her eyes she said, "Well, I own this church."

ROLL CALL

Name _____

Address _____

Member of this church ☐

Member of another church ☐

Please send for my membership at _____

Visitor ☐

Prospective member ☐

Form B. ROLL CALL CARD

Without a moment's hesitation the young usher replied, "Well, lady, I must say, you certainly have a big debt."

The man who meets the visitors at the door may encounter such embarrassments, but they are worth facing to welcome one stranger.

After giving a welcome to the visitor the receptionist takes the visitor to a table in the foyer and introduces him to the "guardian" of the register. For no visitors' register is of much value unless it has someone to watch over it. While the receptionist returns to the door to find the next visitor, the person at the register then guides the visitor in recording his name, residence, church affiliation, and his permanent community. After the visitor moves into the church, the "guardian" checks his name if he thinks it should be placed on the prospect list.

Many of these visitors come to a service to worship only once. They are visiting Aunt Sally, or they are just passing through town and drop in. But many of them are in the community to stay. Let us remember that America is on the march. A vast migration is taking place. The come and go of people never ceases. People are on new farms, in new industries, in apartment houses for the first time, in temporary trailer camps, or in new homes. They feel strange, and yet they want the stability of the church. That they attend a certain church means that they have a religious interest. Record their names!

6. "Hand in names"

Ask the congregation to write down names and addresses of those whom they think should be members of the church. Similar requests in church-school classes, women's societies, and other organizations will keep people on the lookout for new people. Many of these names will already be recorded. But it is better to have a family reported a half dozen times than to miss them just once.

The pastor may request the members to watch for people in their own blocks, across the street, or those who move into the neighborhood. He may ask them to visit and find out if the newcomers are available for the church. A political boss had his henchmen use this plan to keep an entire city in his political grasp, cultivating the new people as they came to the city. Let the sons of light be as wise as the sons of darkness!

7. The pastor's notebook

There are certain contacts which the pastor has, such as weddings, funerals, strangers to whom he is introduced, club and dinner occasions, people in distress or trouble. These afford names for his ever-growing prospect list. It is necessary to do no more than mention this source to the minister who is alert to his primary pastoral responsibility, that of the lost sheep!

8. Check the church membership register

The pastor and one or two individuals in the church who are well acquainted with the community can check the church membership register. You may find that Mrs. Simpson is a church member but has no familiarity with the church school except by remote control and that her husband is not a church member at all. His name was not discovered in the church-school survey because his wife wasn't there. He may think that it is strange that no one from his wife's church has ever even mentioned church membership to him, much less the claim of Christ upon his life. One such man who had no Christian profession, when approached, said, "I've wondered for ten years why no one in my wife's church ever was interested in me."

This extra checking to add to the increasing prospect list is often most rewarding.

9. The census sheet

In some cities and a few towns census sheets are printed by some individual or institution. These sheets list the names and addresses of people who have just moved into the community and sometimes those whose addresses have changed. Occasionally census sheets give the church affiliations of those on the list. It is well to inquire for such a service. The service is printed weekly or biweekly in some communities by the Chamber of Commerce. In certain places the public utilities will furnish on request the names of people who have just made new utility connections.

Some communities have a "Welcome Wagon" which visits new residents with a welcome from certain commercial concerns and gives the information to the patronizing institution. Churches may participate in these services—for a price.

THE PROSPECT LIST

A pertinent question arises: "How is the pastor going to assemble these names and keep this list of prospects for effective use?"

Since the names will be changing constantly, growing and decreasing as people are added and as they are taken into the membership or move away, it is necessary to have a flexible system. The most effective one is a card system, with each family assigned to one card.

The prospect card

A very simple yet inclusive Prospect and Assignment Card is reproduced on page 39 (Form C). It has the dual purpose of both a prospect card for the permanent record and an assignment card for the visitors. These cards may be printed or mimeographed locally, or they may be secured from the Department of Evangelism of the Federal Council of the Churches of Christ in America, or from denominational boards of evangelism.

It is preferable to give the names of the entire family on one card rather than to place each individual on a separate one. The reason for this is that this program of evangelism is primarily through family visitation. We hope to visit a home and at the conclusion be able to say, "This day is salvation come to this house."

This particular type of card makes it possible to check the specific reasons why the name of the person is on the responsibility list. This enables the visitors to have a fairly satisfactory background of the family and its connection with the church as well as a point or two of information with which to begin the interview.

The cards should be made out in duplicate. On the night of visitation the visitors take the orignal and return the duplicate to the pastor after signing it—to guard against loss and to give the pastor a record of assignments.

The prospect files

Each church should have three files of prospects: (1) the Live File; (2) the Postponed File; and (3) the Dead File.

The Live File includes all the names of people who are now prospects for the church and should be called upon at once.

The Postponed File includes the names of those who will not make a decision now but should be seen at a later date. They are the "almost persuaded." This file should be kept chronologically by months. This is similar to the file the insurance agent keeps on you. A minister hardly arrives in town until the insurance agent knocks at the door. The minister welcomes him in, and soon finds out why he has come. He tells the agent that he has all the insurance he can possibly carry and, to settle the matter without too much finality, says, "Well, I might be interested in six months or so." The minister is quite pleased with himself to have got off so easily. But six months from that day into the pastor's study

PROSPECT AND ASSIGNMENT CARD

Name _____

Address _____

REASONS FOR BEING ON OUR RESPONSIBILITY LIST

____ Member of Sunday school   ____ Attends church service
____ Child in Sunday school   ____ Wife or children members
____ Baby on Cradle Roll   ____ Attends some women's meetings
____ Survey—prefer our church   ____ Attends young people's society
____ Member elsewhere   ____ Contributor

Other reasons or information _____

Called on by _____ Date _____

Report and follow-up recommendations _____

_____

_____

_____

_____

FORM C. PROSPECT AND ASSIGNMENT CARD

walks the insurance agent. You put him off, but you didn't get rid of him. According to the pastor's own instructions the agent tucked his name away in his "Postponed File" under date six months later! Insurance agents should be no more interested and effective in selling insurance than pastors are in reaching people for Christ and the church. File the names away for future assignment.

The Dead File does not include the people who are dead. Some in that file may be dead spiritually, but nothing can be done about them. Others may be very much alive. They are the people who, for some very good reason, or for no reason at all, will never become members of your church. They have been visited, and the reason they will not become members of the church calling upon them is indicated on their cards. For instance, they do not belong to that denomination and never intend to—more the pity, the pastor thinks. Or they are moving soon to another city, or they request definitely that no further calls be made upon them.

We have one such card in our Dead File—and it is the reason we decided to have such a file. It reads: "These people say they are Episcopalians but wish their children to attend our church school. They have been solicited for membership twelve times, and they think that is enough." Well, I think that it was too much. They will never become members of our church. Therefore we should not take the time of our visitors nor impose upon these people by calling upon them any more. The Episcopal rector should be given their names. Yet the next time we take a survey of our church school these children will fill out survey cards, and their names will be ready for our prospect files. As we check these names against the Dead File we will discover the reason for not visiting them again.

An up-to-date file of prospects

Cultivating the constituency roll of prospective members requires time, energy, and a little financial outlay. But it is the foundation upon which any visitation evangelism program can be carried through. Detailed clerical work and careful checking are necessary to obtain the names of all the people for whom any church is responsible. If the church isn't too large, an energetic pastor can do this secretarial work himself. Constant and repeated checking is required to prevent duplication and also to see that no single individual is omitted.

Many churches have handicapped themselves because their lists have been only half prepared. If two hundred prospects are interviewed instead of one hundred, other things being equal, twice as many converts and new members will be won.

If a pastor has two hundred adult and youth prospects, including both those for first decision and those for church letter transfers, with twenty visitors he has a set-up that should yield at least fifty to seventy-five new members for his church from the first calls made upon them. Faithful follow-up will yield many more from this group.

CHAPTER III

Securing the Visitors

"How am I going to find people to do this visiting?" asked one minister. "When I call for volunteers my people reply, 'I can't do personal work. You will have to get someone else.'"

It must be confessed that this can be the most difficult part of the entire visitation evangelistic endeavor. But it must also be said that the selection of visitors not only is the key to success but also gives to the pastor the glorious fulfillment of an inner circle of disciples with whom he may feel more closely akin in spiritual seeking than to any of his other parishioners. Enough lay people can always be secured when they are shown that the work is within their powers. If the pastor seeks God's guidance as he carefully prepares his list of solicitors, and then in an intelligent and challenging way presents the invitation to each one of them, there are always some who will respond. He may secure their agreement to serve through their sense of duty and high privilege. But they will soon forget the demands made on them in joyful amazement at the marvelous results they reap of souls harvested from whitened fields.

Two rules must invariably be followed. Any minister who violates them invites disaster and prevents some capable people from ever becoming witnesses for Christ. Any minister who follows them will always secure enough visitors to care for his

SECURING THE VISITORS

responsibility list. These two rules, as inflexible as gravity, are:

1. Do not ask for volunteers.
2. Secure the visitors yourself.

Volunteers will fail

Those who are to be visitors should never be solicited in a public service. This is a sacred and delicate task, and those to perform it should always be sought out individually and personally. The trouble with asking publicly for those who will agree to do this greatest of all services is that at least one person—possibly most of those who offer—will become a candidate not because he is capable but because he is willing or has some extra time on his hands. He will probably turn out to be thoroughly incapable. Accidents happen even in the best of unregulated churches. While a plea for help sometimes calls forth a capable candidate, pastors testify that invariably they have made a serious and embarrassing mistake whenever they have used volunteers.

At a visitation evangelistic campaign in El Paso four of the five co-operating pastors hand-picked their workers several weeks prior to the campaign. But on the Sunday before the opening of the campaign on Monday, one pastor preached a sermon on "Personal Evangelism" and at the close of the sermon called for those who would volunteer to do personal work during the succeeding week. He asked them to come to the altar for dedication. He took an awful chance! With more than one hundred persons in prospect for faith in Christ and membership in his church, he waited until the last moment, and then made a public appeal for workers.

Suppose no one had made a move! Fortunately several devoted members came to the altar and offered themselves as visitors. How many talented people might have proffered their services had they not had previous unbreakable appointments no one will ever know.

At the close of the campaign the pastor admitted his error, saying, "It certainly was fortunate that several consecrated people came forward Sunday. Even at that I didn't get enough. But I had plenty of trouble with one woman. Her tongue was loose at both ends. I placed her with the best worker I had, and she reported tonight in disgust that they had secured no results because her companion talked about everthing except church membership."

Willingness is small qualification for personal visitors. The pastor must convince the majority of his best people that they have the ability and that their first and highest obligation to Christ is to be emissaries for him. They will be people who are busy, who are sensitive, who hesitate to swell the ranks of their obligations, and who must be persuaded that as Christians they have in this a sacred responsibility of first priority as well as a glorious privilege.

A pastor asked a young insurance executive to join his "Fishermen's Club," as he called the visitation evangelistic organization he was forming. He replied, "Preacher, I'll do anything else you ask of me, but I'm no soul-winner. I can't do that."

The pastor asked him, "Why do you sell insurance?"

"Because I believe in it. I think I am rendering a service to a man when I get him to take out protection for his family."

"Do you believe in Christ and the church?" asked the preacher.

"Certainly," replied the layman.

"You believe in insurance enough to solicit people to take it. Do you believe in Christ and your church enough to ask people to accept Christ and join his church?" probed the pastor.

"You've got me, preacher," replied the layman. "Put me down. I'll try it."

The pastor convinced this layman that the work was in line with what he was already doing, but with greater possibilities. And that layman became the rock upon which that pastor built a fellowship of evangelism. He became chairman of that Fishermen's Club, which secured more than a thousand new members for his church, almost half of them on confession of faith.

The pastor's personal responsibility

From visitation endeavors all across America the voice comes with repeated insistence: "Pastor! Select your evangelistic visitors yourself. Personally press them into service."

Prospective visitors will often refuse the solicitation of someone else, but they will not refuse their pastor when he makes a personal request for them to come to the aid of the cause.

The minister knows his people better than anyone else. He appreciates the spiritual and personality qualifications necessary for the most successful visitors. He knows from experience whether individual members evidence in their own lives the Master whom they would present to nonbelievers. He can be discerning as to whether they are the kind of persons to represent the church so that anyone with a membership in another community will be attracted to membership with them.

When a layman agrees to serve, he is asked to sign a covenant agreement (Form D, on the opposite page).

Procedure for selecting visitors

1. *List the most competent people in the church membership.* These people need not have done personal work before. Capable people who have never spoken in public or done religious work, if they have essential qualifications, quickly adjust themselves and develop a contagious evangelistic enthusiasm. They are to receive adequate training. Therefore put on your list every individual whom you think should be recruited under the banner of witnesses for Christ.

2. *List twenty names for each hundred prospect cards in your responsibility list.* Does this appear to be an arbitrary number? It has proved itself by experience with hundreds of churches in visitation campaigns. Out of each twenty members on the list the pastor will secure the consent of about fourteen. Fourteen visitors—that is, seven teams—should

> **VISITATION AGREEMENT**
>
> I agree to participate in the visitation endeavor.
>
> I will attend the suppers and training conferences each evening at 6:15-7:00 P.M., unless prevented by circumstances beyond my control.
>
> I am willing, after receiving instructions, to take a reasonable assignment at each meeting and to have friendly visits with the prospects.
>
> Name_____Telephone_____
>
> Address _____

FORM D. VISITORS AGREEMENT CARD

cover about one hundred visits in four nights in an urban community. In a rural community fewer visits can be made in an evening, and so several more visitors for each one hundred prospects are required.

3. *Call on these prospective visitors* PERSONALLY. A personal call from the pastor means that the pastor thinks it is important enough to do something about it himself. A telephone call is usually less than half effective.

One pastor let himself get behind schedule and thought he was forced to use the telephone. He had personally invited thirty persons to serve. Out of this number he secured twenty-two commitments—a good average. Then the time got the better of him.

He was within a few days of the campaign. He thought he did not have time to call upon the remainder, so he substituted the telephone for the pastoral call. Out of thirty-five telephone calls he secured only eight agreements to serve.

Above everything else, pastor, go personally to the ones you think should do the work and talk it through with them face to face. It is easy to say No to a little black instrument, but it is easy to say Yes to a challenging personal appeal for a great cause.

4. *Secure more men than women.* A few churches use only men. Men will get more decisions than women with the same number of prospects because men are accustomed to directness and to gaining decisions in business and in trading. Men habitually use the direct method of selling, and therefore they proceed immediately to securing decisions. Of course there are exceptions to this rule. Many women make excellent evangelistic visitors. Some women are more skillful than men in securing commitments. An efficient team of women is better than a weak team of men. But always secure as many capable men as possible.

5. *Secure middle-aged and young people.* Generally speaking, they are more effective than older people. The best workers on the average come from the ages twenty-five to fifty. Exceptions turn up in every church. Unusual personalities sometimes become the rule. The best man in a city campaign was sixty-eight. One woman who admitted she was "on the rise of sixty" was very sincere, direct, and win-

some. She and her partner are still continuing to win people.

Married couples prove very effective in family visitation. One church in a new residential section of a large city used only young married couples. They secured dozens of young couples who were moving into the new homes of their community.

6. *Draft your visitors.* Don't ask them to serve. They know what drafting is. It is the call of something so important and so urgent that refusals are not accepted. Simply say that this is the most important work of your church this year. It is the greatest service they can possibly render to Christ and their church. Tell them that you have selected them because you know they can do this work well and in the proper spirit. If someone persists in his feeling of inadequacy, ask him to serve one week experimentally, with the promise that if at the end of this endeavor he still feels it is beyond his powers then in any further endeavors you will not call upon him. If someone has a real reason for not serving, accede to it. But few will turn you down. Men will accept this high call to an allegiance beyond their accustomed easy ways if the challenge is as Tertullian wrote of the ardent early Christians: "These persecutions do not worry us, for we have joined this church fully accepting the terms of its agreement with us, as men whose very souls are not our own."

7. *Get their agreement three or four weeks in advance.* Many of the busiest and most effective workers cannot respond on short notice. They will have

previous engagements. Few people can give a good excuse for not accepting an invitation three weeks in the future—especially one of such high urgency.

8. *Get their agreement to attend every session of suppers and conferences.* It is imperative that every worker be present at every one of the four sessions. The pastor will conduct a school of instruction. These pupils cannot learn the technique of effective invitation in absentia. Visitors secure more decisions the second and third evenings than they do the first night. Inviting people to become followers of Jesus Christ and to unite with the church is too important to be done haphazardly. Regular attendance provides enlarging information about how to visit effectively, and experience in actual visitation. "Study to show thyself approved unto God, a workman that needeth not to be ashamed." Regular attendance at every session is necessary for graduation as a master in visitation evangelism. If a person cannot attend every night, find someone else.

A high calling

Never once let a worker think of this service as trivial. If there is one impression that is necessary in the mind of the modern churchman it is the urgency of this hour, the imperative need for humanity to have salvation through the life and pattern of the Master. There is potency in the words and message which the visitors carry from home to home, for the "precious jeopardy" of a life or a family may be dependent upon their witnessing.

SECURING THE VISITORS

Frank Crane once said, "It takes so little to make people happy. Just a touch, if we know how to give it, just a word fitly spoken, a slight readjustment of some bolt or pin or bearing in the delicate machinery of a soul." The right word, spoken in the right spirit and under the impulse of the right purpose, has upon countless occasions changed the destiny of life. This is the glorious opportunity; for God is working by the side of each witness, supplying strength, wisdom, guidance. With God's help we can meet our opportunities victoriously.

Pray the Lord of the harvest

Here is an unbelievable record. The wisest and best of all men, who above all others knew the hearts of men, could not choose his own associates without help.

On the night before the Master chose twelve men to become the intimate nucleus which would grow into the Christian Church, he spent the entire night in prayer. He sought God's guidance. It is quite apparent that this was not the first thought Jesus entertained that he should have an inner circle of disciples. It is also evident that there must have been more than twelve men from whom to choose, possibly a score. There may have been a hundred. We know the names of the twelve. But we do not know the names of the "almost" disciples.

How well Jesus chose we know, for those men became the persons through whom the new life of Christ was disseminated and spread abroad. They became the rock upon which the church was built.

Yet, even with such fervent spiritual selection followed by such adequate training, one of these men proved insufficient, even a traitor.

In the choosing of our inner circle of visitors how much more than our Master should we, who are merely human ministers, go to God in prayer! Let us lift up into the Holy Presence of God through our intercession these men and women whom in our judgment we think can become effective lay evangelists. He will give direction where we grope and are indecisive. Frequently he will lead us to the right person whom we had not thought about at all. Even before we have approached individuals to ask them to serve, the Holy Spirit will be found intercedingfor us in his holy cause. Let us therefore prepare our lists of possible visitors in the white light of the Holy Spirit's guidance.

The actual visits to solicit the aid of laymen should be made as though we walked the streets of our town keeping step to music heard from far above it. Urgency attends the pastor who seeks to draft men to what has become a highest and holiest service. Under the leading of the Spirit of God we may be confident that the Lord of the harvest will direct us to the laborers worthy to be hired for divine wages.

As Paul Scherer says, "The world is swung on its hinges, not as much by people who have both feet on the ground as by people who have 'one foot in heaven'!"

CHAPTER IV

Using Trained Visitors

THERE IS A NEW KIND OF GATHERING AT THE CHURCH tonight. It is Monday, and the pastor, Gideon-like, has chosen about one tenth of his members to attend. It seems like any church supper, except that these members have been divided into pairs, a husband and wife, a couple of young businessmen, two brothers, and so around the group. The time is six fifteen, and the meal begins promptly. The atmosphere is one of expectancy and adventure.

While the people are eating, the pastor moves among them giving to each couple six or eight cards on which are recorded the names and addresses of people who might become new members of their church. These cards are grouped geographically so that calls upon them can be made with no waste of time.

At six thirty the pastor asks those who have not finished their meal to continue quietly, but to give close attention. In a most illuminating manner he presents the art of winning people. His talk consists of a most interesting explanation of the way in which each one of these laymen can secure decisions for the Christian life. The instruction is thorough but brief. It closes at exactly seven five, at which time the meeting breaks up and each team leaves immediately to proceed with the visiting. Each couple makes friendly calls in three or four homes—with amazing results.

A WORKABLE PLAN OF EVANGELISM

On the three succeeding nights the teams come back for supper and more pastoral instruction in what these laymen have now discovered is a wonderful art and a great joy. They have been successful in helping others make decisions for Christ! There is a buoyancy of spirit and an exultant gladness in the soul of a man when he is able to introduce his friends to the Best Friend. They enthusiastically report that the Holy Spirit has led them to banish modern devils which have beset contemporary people. Like the seventy of old, they rejoice not only in spiritual mastery but above all that new names are enrolled in heaven!

ADEQUATE PREPARATION

But this series of supper meetings and the results did not just happen. The movement originated with the pastor. For several weeks he had prepared for these few days of harvest. First there was the preparation of the soil, then the planting, then the cultivating, and now the harvest. For several months the pastor had directed the surveys which provided the prospects. He had personally interviewed and secured commitments of all those who were present at the supper meetings. And he had made careful and thorough preparation for the instruction for each night.

This pastor and other pastors whose people win the largest number of converts, and whose work is most lasting, follow certain tested procedures.

USING TRAINED VISITORS

1. Prospect and Assignment Cards

After the surveys have been made, the names of each family of prospects are listed on a Prospect and Assignment Card (Form C, page 39). These should be made in duplicate. This can be done on the typewriter with a carbon sheet.

Every team of visitors should be given both the original and duplicate of each family. The visitors should keep the originals and return the duplicates to the pastor with their own names written upon them. This is very important, for in spite of their good intentions some visitors will lose or misplace cards. Women have too many pocketbooks. Men have more than one suit of clothes. And some people are born careless. Visitors may lose some cards, but if the pastor has the signed duplicates and checks them with the reports no person's card will be misplaced or lost. Human nature being what it is, if the visitors know the pastor is keeping a check upon them they will do better work.

2. The number of prospects to assign

Cards for six to eight families should be given to each team. People do not stay at home when we want to call upon them; with six or eight assignments each team should find at least three families at home on the first night.

Each night the pastor finds the needs of each team and adds new assignment cards in the same neighborhood. One team may solicit three families the first night. Three or four new families in the same territory should be assigned the second night. Some team may find everybody away the first night. On the second evening they should try again without additional assignments. These wanderers will return home sometime!

3. Geographical assignments

The pastor will take care to arrange the group of prospect cards in as nearly the same neighborhood as possible. This saves time in going from place to place. It may make a difference of five to twenty new members in a week. It will also conserve the visitors' energies and will put them to the kingdom's use instead of wearing out tires or shoe leather and patience.

4. Special assignments

Certain unchurched individuals in every community require special care. Jesus gave more attention to Peter than he did to some of the other disciples, possibly because he needed more. Nowhere in the Bible do we find that one individual is more important in the sight of God than any other. Yet an individual may be far more valuable to the Kingdom of God than another. As Peter he may become a "Prince of Apostles."

Certain people are hard to catch. Assign them to an expert fisherman. Some people have greater influence in the community than others. Send the most persuasive visitors to them. Every minister knows some particular "hardened sinner" in his community who, if redeemed, would shake that whole community to its foundations, so that perhaps a number of his cronies in sin would follow him into the Kingdom. Some man who has won the victory over sin and death should be sent to see him—instead of letting his name fall into a neighborhood group to be covered by that sincere and friendly young couple, Mr. and Mrs. Justmarried, who united with the church last month, and who have never grappled in the dark fight to the death.

Again there are some people who can be of great usefulness to the church and the Kingdom. Here is a young man who would be a fine leader of young people. Or there is a public school teacher who could take that primary department whose superintendent moved away six weeks ago. Or here is a man of wealth. What about him. The church has sometimes been rightly accused of preferring the rich to the poor, of catering to those who have influence over those who have little or none. But I do not remember that Jesus turned the rich young ruler away because he possessed a fortune. Instead Jesus looked upon him, loved him, and immediately assessed the value of his wealth for others. When the rich young man turned away, two were sorrowful, Jesus as well as he. It is interesting that everything Jesus said and did had to do with human hearts. The soul of a rich man is as important—but no more so—as the soul of a poor man. But if a man will consecrate his wealth to the service of the Kingdom he can do much for the salvation of souls and the conversion of the world.

Whenever any man has special problems or can

have unusual value for Christ, give that man the greatest care in winning him. Give him the most capable visitors to call upon him.

When Frank Crandall joined the church, the whole community was startled out of its moral lethargy. For he became a power for God. Others who had accompanied him in sin found him still their companion, but now to reclaim them. When the orphanage was built, he was the greatest personality in support of the parentless children. His was the influence that built the men's class to over a hundred in attendance. Everybody agreed that Frank Crandall would never have accepted Christ's way—at least for years he never had—by any other influence than that of his best friend, a true Christian man, whom the pastor asked to call upon him for a decision.

5. Written reports

Written reports must be made upon every prospect card returned by a team. Specific instructions should be given by the pastor that each decision and rejection must be explained in writing. To this there should be no exceptions. The visitors will write the report of the interview on the front or back of the card and sign their names. Memories fade, and oral reports cannot all be remembered by the pastor.

One pastor trusted what he thought was an excellent memory, but the fickle lady deceived him. There were thirty names, various excuses, some acceptances, one or two later calls, all of which blurred into a confusing fog. He wasted the next night's precious period trying to straighten out what written reports would have made accurate and permanent.

No time is available at the suppers to explain various situations. Written reports are the only solution. If the pastor needs further information, he can telephone the visitors, since their names are signed to the cards.

6. Pastor's instruction period

As Jesus gave specific guidance to his seventy evangelists, the pastor conducts a thirty-minute instruction period so that his workers may become effective and persuasive in their interviews. This period must be zealously safeguarded from interruptions or distractions. It is a sacred time. It is holy ground. This central feature of the program will be set forth in the next chapter and in Part II.

7. Membership Sunday

The second Sunday after the visitation campaign closes should be designated as Membership Sunday. All persons who indicate their willingness to unite with the church should be requested to present themselves on this day. The reason the second Sunday is chosen instead of the next one is that it will give the pastor time to visit the newly won individuals and also to enable the follow-up of indecisive cases. The value of having all who intend to unite with the church come into the membership at the same time is apparent.

Some pastors and some denominations may have other arangements or ritual for the reception of new members. Of course each pastor will announce this to his group of workers.

A WORKABLE PLAN OF EVANGELISM

VARIOUS PLANS FOR VISITATION EVANGELISM

There are several plans of visitation evangelism, each adapted to a specific situation. Evangelism is not a matter of one week or one campaign. Every church should have a year-around plan that will not end until the last and the least person has been won. Churches in scattered rural communities cannot operate in the same fashion as churches in compact town or metropolitan areas. This program of visitation evangelism has such adaptabilities that each church may use the method most suited to reach the most people in its community.

Experience has proved that the shorter the course of instruction the larger the results. Thus a more compact scheme should be used wherever possible.

1. The one-week campaign

The visitors are to be trained as interviewing witnesses for Christ not only for one brief campaign, however effective that may be, but also for the ensuing year, yes, the remainder of their lives. It is advisable that the one-week campaign be used first. Variations of visitation evangelism may be projected later as they suit the development of evangelism in the particular church and community. Experience all across America has proved that the largest results are attained by a one-week campaign, meeting each night, Monday through Thursday. It is the fundamental program, with which any pastor or church should first begin.

The visitors meet at the church for supper, served by women of the church who are not going to visit.

USING TRAINED VISITORS

They should not attempt to make any profit on the meals, this being their service to the winning of people to Christ. The supper should be served at the lowest cost. No price should be charged which would keep any visitors from attending. Many churches pay for the suppers out of the church treasury. What a cheap price for a revival! The food served should be simple, for the purpose of the lunch is not that the diners may enjoy a meal or even have fellowship during the week, but rather that it may be convenient for people to gather early and be out visiting at the earliest possible moment. If a dessert is served, let it be placed on the table *before* the meal, and let no dishes be removed prior to adjournment. Time is too precious for anything but the instructions and the calling.

The supper is essential. Any pastor who thinks he can get his people to come to the church by six thirty after getting their own evening meals at home merely needs to try it to learn it is entirely impractical.

The time for the supper is six fifteen—no later! Request the visitors to gather if at all possible at six o'clock, to be seated immediately, to have their reports ready if they can do so before coming, and to be through eating by six thirty. It is important that the women have the meal ready no later than the time set. This may all seem like undue haste, but this urgency is required so that no time shall be taken from the primary business at hand.

The schedule is as follows:

    6:15—Supper

6:25—Reports
6:35—Instructions by the pastor
7:05—Dismissal, and immediate adjournment to visit the prospects

The one-week campaign has values that one of longer duration cannot possibly possess. It maintains a keen interest for the visitors. They will set aside four days and work more effectively and with less loss of interest than if calls are scattered out over a longer period. This is a school of instruction based upon two factors, instruction and practice. The instruction is followed by an attempt to put the teaching into practice. The visitors will gain some success, possibly have some failures, and probably make some mistakes. They will come back the following evening eager to learn why such things happened or failed to happen, and wanting to know more about this wonderful experience. Their memories will be fresh concerning the previous night. The pastor can catch any discouragement before it has time to set in their minds. The report period will give the less successful visitors encouragement, refreshment, and new determination.

A most successful campaign with amazing results can be conducted in four nights.

2. On the circuit: one week in each church

"Such a plan for a one-week campaign is all right for a minister who has just one church, but what about those of us who have three or four churches?" asked a pastor on a four-church circuit.

Visitation evangelism is being carried on just as

successfully in charges of from three to six or seven churches as in those of just one church. There are two plans.

One pastor with three churches describes in this fashion how he does it: "I carry on a one-week campaign in my first church. The next week I go to the second church for a similar campaign. The third week I have a campaign in the last church. I have made my preparation in advance in each instance, and in three weeks I have had a regular evangelistic visitation in every one of my churches."

There is a second alternative in which the pastor can carry on the program simultaneously throughout his several churches.

3. Once a week for four weeks

A visitation program may be conducted on the exact principles of the one-week campaign, except that the visitors meet one night each week for four weeks. The plan is set up on the same basis and with the same program as the one-week campaign, except that the meetings are held on the same night of each week. For instance, four Monday evenings are used. The same schedule for the evenings is conducted. The supper each Monday is at six fifteen, followed by the instruction, closing at seven five.

This method of meeting once a week is very successful where a pastor has several churches under his charge. If the pastor prefers not to have a one-week visitation campaign in each community, he can meet with the visitors of one church on Monday night, the second church on Tuesday night, the third on Wednesday night, the fourth on Thursday night, giving to each the first evening's instructions. The visitors make their calls on the prospects following the instruction meeting. The second week the pastor repeats his rounds, giving the second instruction. The third and fourth weeks conclude the program.

A variation of this plan is for the group of visitors to meet following the midweek service for forty-five minutes, then make the calls the next night. Let us say the midweek service is held on Wednesday at seven thirty. At eight thirty, following the devotional service, the pastor calls his visitors together. No one should attend this meeting except the appointed visitors or else there will be some who feel compelled to participate but are not competent to do this kind of calling. The pastor pairs the visitors, gives them the assignments, receives their brief reports, and gives them their instructions for the evening. On Thursday night they make the calls on those assigned to them. The following Wednesday the group of visitors meet again after the midweek service, make their reports, and receive new assignments and further instructions. This continues each Wednesday and Thursday for four weeks.

In a large city church we have tried this once-a-week method with a group of women who meet at ten o'clock each Tuesday morning for a month preceding Easter. The women make their calls in the afternoons. There is one unsatisfactory element in afternoon visiting, and that is that the men are seldom at home. Calls are much more effective if they can be made when the entire family is at home. We have secured satisfactory results by assigning to these afternoon visitors only women prospects.

A pastor should choose this once-a-week plan only if he is convinced it will produce larger results than the one-week program. A fine combination is to put on an intensive one-week campaign where the interest is held to the one objective of winning people to Christ, and then to follow up the succeeding year with a meeting one night each week at some season such as Easter.

Still another variation is to meet on alternate nights, Monday and Wednesday for instruction, and Tuesday and Thursday for visiting. Two such weeks would suffice.

4. Once a month

The last and certainly the least desirable adaptation of the initial program is to have the visitors meet once each month. If the other two plans are entirely impractical, this substitute is a last resort. Its disadvantages are apparent. No school would operate with a class once a month. Too much time elapses between the instructions and the next meetings. The visitors who have not had success the first night become almost hopelessly discouraged. And yet some churches have used this plan with moderate success—enough so that if the other plans cannot be put into operation this one is worth the effort.

5. Church-school evangelism

As everyone knows, many of the church members are brought into membership through the church school. The information and technique of visitation evangelism should be known by the faculty of the church school. They should know how to lead each pupil, boy or girl as well as man or woman, into a personal relationship of devoted discipleship to Jesus Christ and into faithful church membership. Teachers not in a school of evangelism may be instructed by the pastor in two periods. The instructions described in the second part of this book under the titles "Securing the Decision," "Efficient Visiting," and "Family Evangelism" may be combined for these two sessions. If it is very difficult to get the faculty together more than once, the discussion can be abbreviated into a one-hour period.

About five weeks before Easter on a certain evening I called together all the teachers and officers of the young people's and adult classes. Special effort was exerted to have everyone there. All except one were present. The Prospect and Assignment Cards for each class were presented to the teacher and president. They were told that these were members of their classes who were not members of our church. It was explained that the responsibility for winning these people would be theirs and that those present would be expected to see each prospect personally within the next two weeks. I then spent an hour giving a combination of "Efficient Visiting" and "Family Evangelism," and some of the excuses offered.

The teacher of one of these adult classes was a fine Christian man, but neither he nor his wife was a member of our congregation. While they were faithful in their responsibilities, they had never transferred their membership to our church. The next Sunday this teacher used the class period with his adult class of men and women, telling them very much of what I had told them about primary loyalty to Christ. He explained to them the necessity of hurdling excuses and of identifying oneself with the congregation where one is attending. He told them that he and his wife were transferring their memberships and that each nonmember would be visited in the next two weeks. He said he hoped that Easter would find every one of them members of our church.

The visitation proved so successful and the enthusiasm grew to such an extent that they decided not to wait until Easter but to unite with the church immediately. On the third Sunday before Easter the entire class sat together. At the close of the service this teacher, his wife, and fourteen men and women from their class were received into the fellowship of the church, where they have since been most faithful and active. Of this group three men and four women became Christian disciples for the first time. The wife of one of these men was overjoyed and later said to the pastor, "For years I have hoped that someday my husband would become an avowed Christian and unite with the church. The personal invitation brought him over. He is making some changes in his way of living. I don't think anything else would ever have won him."

Every church-school teacher and officer should be trained as an effective visitor to secure definite Christian decisions.

6. The continuation program

When a church has a select and trained group of workers, it is then possible to plan a regular program of evangelism which will continue indefinitely and constantly beyond the initial campaign. At the last meeting the pastor should propose a continuation plan. These visitors have climbed to the height of the mountain of achieved inspiration. The pastor now points out the vista before them. From the vantage of the mount of vision they will see stretching ahead fields still white to the harvest. They will see that the work has just been started. Many prospects were not at home and were not seen. Others need further cultivation before making a decision. New prospects will constantly be found. These visitors who have tasted the fruits of victory will not be satisfied to see such fine work stopped. Under the challenging inspiration they will readily volunteer for further service. Effectiveness in this service depends upon the attitude of the worker. He must be brought to feel that his is a sacred trust which he is privileged to fulfill for the benefit of others and the glory of God. The pastor should propose a definite program to recruit new members constantly during the year.

The "Fishermen's Club."—Churches have various names for their permanent evangelistic organizations. In our congregation we have had a "Fishermen's Club" which has met regularly for some years. Its members have won hundreds of people. The last time, we were together for two nights for supper and visiting. In those two nights of calling they secured forty-one new members, eighteen of whom were on profession of faith. They secured favorable decisions from 65 per cent of the prospects interviewed. This Fishermen's Club is composed entirely of men. However, most churches include both men and women. In some churches the organization is known as the "Fellowship of Evangelism," or "Christ's Witnesses."

One night a month.—The plan most widely used is for the visitors to meet one night each month for assignments, further instruction, discussion of the spirit and methods of the work, and two or more hours of visiting. The time set may be either after the Sunday night church service or following the midweek service. Incidentally it will be a stimulus for attendance at these services, if stimulation is needed! The best time is the third week of the month. Prospects gathered during the preceding month or left over from previous calling are assigned. The visitors may wish to call more than one night, but each team is requested not to take more than the three nights. The reports are made and concluded the following Sunday night or at the close of the next midweek service. Brief reports should be made publicly at the meetings by a few teams which have been successful. The visitors are not called upon to serve again for a month. They work one half a week and rest three and a half weeks. Alternation of intense activity and long rest maintains the zest of the work. The first Sunday of each month is then Membership Sunday.

7. Special evangelistic services

The trouble with most evangelistic revival services in these days is that there are no personal workers. Stepping across the aisle to ask a man if he is a Christian in most places just isn't being done any more. The failure of people personally to solicit nonmembers during revival services is one of the reasons for the usual ineffectiveness of special meetings. Men fail to become seekers for the strayed and lost not because they do not have the talents and abilities but because they do not have the information and inspiration to carry out the highest discipleship to which they are called.

If the church has a group of trained visitors who know how to win people, then whenever special evangelistic preaching services are held they can be sent out in teams of two. They can call upon the prospective members with real assurance of success. The visiting may be done prior to the evening services, in the mornings, in the afternoons, or even at mealtime. The reports may be made following the services. New assignments may then be given to be called upon during the following day.

8. Special services following visitation campaign

The finest development that is coming out of the visitation evangelistic program is a combination of the visiting with special preaching worship services. Undoubtedly many of those who are won in the visitation need the reinforcement to their faith which comes from earnest, sincere preaching. Practically every one of them will have had enough background out of which to make a decision. Nevertheless, the preaching of the Word of God and the corporate worship with other people will be of great inspiration and encouragement.

One church in a Western state conducted a one-week visitation campaign. During that week decisions were made. When people were undecided and not ready to commit themselves, they were told that beginning the third Sunday there would be morning and evening preaching services for a week. They were invited to attend. While no pressure was put upon them in the services, during that week more people made their decisions. Those who were won during the visitation were also invited to attend the special services. Here the dedications which they had made in private were deepened and strengthened. On Membership Sunday 240 members were received into that church. Month by month the continuation program has been followed, and the new members received into that church during the year reached the unbelievable total of 508.

This plan may be a solution for the pastor who wishes to hold both visitation and evangelistic services. One week is devoted to visitation evangelism. After an intermission of two or three weeks there follows a week, or it may be two weeks, of preaching services. This interval of a half month or more is used for personal visits by the pastor to those who have made commitments and for call-backs by the visitors on those needing further attention.

The special preaching services can be planned so as to deepen the convictions of those who have made their decisions during the visitation. They may be the seal of renewed spiritual commitments and life dedication.

A serious danger must be recognized and presented to the visitors during the visitation. It is easy to ask people to attend the special services. This must *not be done at all*—until the end of an interview. Visitors call only for decisions for Christ and for transfers of membership until the decision is made; then in the last moments of the visit the invitation is given to attend the special services. If this danger is not avoided, the visitation will result merely in pleasant propaganda visits without commitments.

9. Year-around evangelism

As a Gothic cathedral presents to the eye and soul a perfect plan of ecclesiastical architecture, so a comprehensive program of evangelism will be pleasing to the sight of God and man as new disciples are received into the Christian fellowship constantly during the year. In some churches the first Sunday of each month will be designated as Membership Sunday. Rarely will a month pass without additions to the congregation. Other churches will be adding new members every Sunday.

The great religious seasons present special opportunities. One pastor has a one-week visitation four times each year, just before Easter, Mother's Day, World Communion Sunday, and Christmas. With such a program and consecrated work no church could possibly go through a year without adding to the faith those who are being saved.

10. Special assignments

Fishing is a fine art whether one makes his livelihood catching the piscatorial variety or whether, as Jesus taught his disciples, one enters the desperately serious business of fishing for men. Certain people are not difficult to catch. They seem to be waiting for someone to do little more than cast in their direction. Immediately they strike, requesting the transfer of membership or promptly confirming a decision to discipleship. But there are certain persons who are wary, who frighten easily, who are determined not to "get hooked," as they would call it. They do not realize that to be captured by Christ is not to lose but to find life. They need as expert attention to every detail as a true fisherman gives to game fish.

John J. Henderson moves to town. The pastor is uncertain as to how he must be approached, whether he will be difficult or easy to win. The pastor has learned to take no chances. There is no visitation campaign on. It has been two months since the last one, and it will be a couple of weeks before the visitors meet again. But there is a man who took the instructions in visitation evangelism and who has been very successful in winning people to Christ. The pastor telephones this man and says, "Mr. John J. Henderson has moved into our community. Here is his background as we have it: . . . He and his family ought to become members of our church. I would appreciate your going by to win him. How about taking Frank Jacobs with you!" And so the pastor has readily at hand men and women trained, effective, and consecrated to the Master. They are ready to begin fishing the moment a prospect appears in the waters of the community.

11. Assumed responsibility

When these evangelistic visitors catch the spirit and feel the responsibility, they will joyfully be on the alert for prospects. Such seeking has just come to fruition. About a year ago I went to the home of a fine young couple who should by all rights be members of our congregation. Their memberships were not even in the same church, although they had children six and ten. They had not transferred their memberships in a dozen years, since before their marriage. For years they had been of no value back in the old churches, and they meant practically nothing in the church life of our community. Like veterans of previous wars, their present value was merely conversational. The visit of the pastor was appreciated, but it produced no results. Nor did a repeat call.

Then on last Sunday morning this couple came forward and united with our church. I might have thought that my visits had produced the harvest. Instead they had been merely seed sowing. On Saturday night I received a telephone call from one of the men, a member of our Fishermen's Club who regularly goes out in visiting. This is what he said, "Mr. and Mrs. McHenry are uniting with our church at the morning service. They have been attending occasionally since you called. My wife and I went over to see them last week and secured their decisions. I wanted you to know about it so you could be expecting them."

The possibilities of this method of personal interviews inaugurated by Jesus are unlimited for the evangelization of men and also for the growth in grace of his followers who witness for him. Jesus depended upon his disciples to spread the Word of God and win converts to his way of life. "As thou hast sent me into the world, even so have I also sent them into the world." Christians who believe sincerely will earnestly and faithfully lead others to know him. Their hearts will be courageous and their feet quick to make straight the highway of God into the souls of men.

CHAPTER V

Training the Visitors

WE NOW COME TO THE MOST VITAL AND ESSENTIAL PART of this entire evangelistic program, the training of the visitors.

When Jesus called Peter and Andrew, he said, "Come ye after me, and I will make you TO BECOME fishers of men." These fishermen knew that fishing is a difficult task at best and that men must work hard and learn to become skilled in the pursuit of the elusive fish. Jesus did not say that he would perform a miracle which would suddenly transform them into men proficient in snatching men's souls from the sea of despair. Had Jesus said to them that instantly and magically they would be changed into fishermen in the new Kingdom, they would have doubted his leadership. But when he asked them to follow him in learning to become fishers of men, they readily accepted and started the three-year course which enabled them to spread the gospel further in their generation than any similar group in history. In this time of discipline and seasoning they became the flaming evangels of the early church.

Anyone who thinks that consecration and willingness are the only qualifications required before asking others to share in the Christian life has much to learn from Jesus. He did not think so. The training of the twelve first fishers of men was long and, even under the Master Teacher, required much instruction and great patience on his part. When we remember that Jesus took several years to train the disciples we shudder to think that we attempt to train capable visiting evangelists in four half-hour periods.

But for our encouragement there are two facts. Jesus evidently gave adequate instruction to the seventy in a short, concise course, perhaps on a single occasion. Also the training course in visitation evangelism is the experience of many pastors and evangelistic leaders developed and refined through many years. The dross has been purged away, and the four lessons in the art of winning people to Christian discipleship contains little extraneous matter. Further development should make them even more pertinent.

It is just as necessary to train our people to become modern fishers of men as it was with Jesus. The present-day church is committed to an educational program. Not only must the church educate its entire congregation in personal and social Christian living, but for those who are to win others to Jesus' way there must be added an intensive course in effective present-day evangelism.

The basic element for the visitors is their own faith, nurtured by the church and taught by the church school. Not one of these visitors ought to be selected unless the pastor is convinced that he is an example of Christian living; for the unchurched will say in their hearts, "What you are speaks so loud I cannot hear what you say." We should also remember that one of the principal by-products of such evangelistic calling will be the deepening of the spiritual life of these visitors. Helping men come to God through personal encounters brings a confident knowledge of being the means through which God has loosed his transforming power. Persons who successfully do this interviewing and find people responding to their invitations will discover their own faith validated in the same way that a minister is renewed in spirit when people unite with the church under his preaching.

Urgency of careful training

By careless approach or unthought or unweighed words it is altogether possible to turn a man permanently away from Christ. Many a visit is made, good things are said, but nothing comes of it. No sales executive would send out agents without giving them careful training. He would feel that his product is too valuable to be sold by incompetent people. Should we consider that the gospel of Jesus Christ is of such nature that it makes no difference who presents it or how carelessly a human soul is approached? The Holy Spirit can take some terribly poor efforts by ineffective and even insincere human agents and transform their pitiable inadequacies into glorious results. We have all seen that happen. But the Spirit of God had to flow through badly choked channels. Often in such instances it never flows through. God forbid that we should ever allow such exceptions to make us careless in presenting the claim of our holy religion. Nothing upon this earth deserves such sincere and effective presentation as the invitation to become a follower of Jesus

Christ. It deserves the best trained as well as the most consecrated ambassadors.

"Study to shew thyself approved unto God, a workman that needeth not to be ashamed." The foundation upon which we can build our evangelism is a group of ministers who know how to teach their laity, and laymen who have studied the best methods of winning disciples. How fine it is to have a human agent acquainted with the Christlike life, knowing in what ways the human spirit responds, what handicaps it has, and how these may be overcome for commitments to right living! How excellent for the Spirit of God to have a human agent who is a clear channel for the spiritual influences to flow into an unregenerate will or neglected life! Results show that an untrained group of visitors going out may secure one or two decisions, often none, in ten calls, while trained and effective callers always average from three to seven decisions in the same number of interviews. One group of Negro visitors in Philadelphia secured decisions of 79 per cent of all prospects visited. One team of two secured eighteen favorable decisions from eighteen called upon.

If there were a group of consecrated laymen trained in effective visitation evangelism in every Protestant church in America, and each church were carrying on a regular annual program, church membership could be increased fifty per cent. This estimate is not based upon guesswork but upon the effectiveness of those who are now projecting such programs. There are not enough ministers in the land personally to win the people to Christ, even if it were advisable for them to do so; but there are enough devoted laymen, if they were properly and adequately trained, to bring the great revival. In this way each generation has in its trust the next generation. If the future is to be Christian, it is through consecrated followers of Jesus who are helping to make the vital presence of the living Christ real to others. The capacity and responsibility to duplicate itself has been the process of Christianity since apostolic days. Jesus said, "Go ye into all the world, and preach the gospel to every creature." The Christian Church will fail in its obligations to the world of today and tomorrow unless there is developed a greater passion for souls. There is too much unconcern for the unconverted!

"Ye shall receive power, after that the Holy Ghost is come upon you: and ye shall be witnesses unto me."

The training course

The physical framework into which a training program can be fitted has been presented. The minister can give a thorough course of training covering the principal features of visiting for decisions in four sessions of thirty minutes each. Such a course will cover the necessary and basic instruction by which laymen can learn to present effectively the claims of Christ and expect definite, favorable decisions. Even after the first instruction period visitors will be moderately successful, and after several training periods they can become self-confident and much more effective.

TRAINING THE VISITORS

Instruction and practice

The training program is planned like certain trade schools with two sections. The pupils spend part of their time in classrooms and part in actual work in the trade. In such schools they attend classes in the mornings and work in the shop in the afternoons.

In similar fashion the evangelistic visitors learn by instruction and by practice. "If any man willeth to do his will, he shall know of the teaching." The teaching part of this evangelistic program is the half-hour instruction given by the pastor, the supper being merely a convenient method of getting together early in the evening. The doing of God's will part consists of two or more hours of putting into practice what has been learned. The doing of God's will in witnessing to others brings as much knowledge of what to do and what is detrimental as the instruction itself.

One man came back after the second night of visiting with the comment, "I got my man tonight. Last night the pastor said, 'Don't argue!' but before I knew it we were in a useless argument and I was urging it on. Then I remembered, 'Don't argue!' and changed the theme back to the man's own commitment. Before long we had his agreement. Then the rest of the family were easy."

The visitor discovered in actual experience what the instruction alone would probably never have clinched. The very night he received his instruction he made it his own by experience. Instruction and actual visiting combine to make successful evangelistic visitors.

A WORKABLE PLAN OF EVANGELISM

The second night there is a brief period of from five to eight minutes to get reports and to allow individuals to raise questions. Through these heartening reports the less successful visitors are encouraged. They are reassured of the efficacy of the method.

The second instruction is more important and thrilling. It portrays a more advanced technique of evangelistic visiting. Having attempted the work the previous evening, the visitors start the second night with more confidence and enthusiasm, feeling that God is giving the increase, and continually testing the instruction by their own experiences. Four such evenings of illuminating description accompanied by trial and error in visiting produce enthusiastic and successful personal workers.

Here, then, is the urgency which requires each visitor to attend *every one* of the instruction and visitation periods. This double necessity is the reason each one should be told emphatically that this is a school of training, not a fellowship supper nor a series of addresses. He might miss a sermon occasionally, but he cannot afford to miss a single one of these evening instruction periods. Each instruction period is entirely different, and each one is exceedingly important. No visitor can qualify at his best unless he is attentively present every night.

The pastor's responsibility

The responsibility for the instructions is entirely upon the pastor. He must give the course of instruction. While there are a few instances where churches or communities can bring in some outside minister who has had experience in training evangelistic workers, in most churches this responsibility is his. And it is within the ability of any pastor, if he will apply himself, to learn to train his lay people in this kind of work. With the great harvest depending upon trained workers to go into the fields to gather it, the pastor must not only pray the Lord of the harvest to send workers but also add works to his faith and prepare himself to guide his laymen.

It is strange that ministers should have so little confidence in themselves and in the power of Christ. Yet the most serious obstacle with most pastors is the fear that they may fail. As in swimming, the only way for the pastor to learn is to get into the water.

The instruction talks in the second section of this book have been so carefully developed by experience that they will yield the desired results. Any minister can master them. He needs only to give the proper study and thoroughly to criticize himself both before and after a presentation.

Often both the minister and his people pioneer together in this field of evangelism. The first attempt, like the first sermon, may not be as fruitful as later and more experienced efforts. And yet most pastors have had unbelievable results in their first visitation campaigns. Minister and people venture together with faith, for they do not their own bidding, but are the servants of the Most High God. God always gives the increase, sometimes thirty-, sixty-, even a hundredfold. I have never yet heard of one of these visitation efforts that was unsuccessful where the pastor was faithful in both preparation and presentation.

The pastor may need to catch a new vision of the high privilege of his calling. Today offers a tremendous challenge to the Christian Church. The impact of a yearning, seeking world must strike his soul with peculiar force. As the shepherd of a church flock he may lead his people to take their faith and share it so that it will reign over the hearts of men. Changed men and women can change a world of warfare into the way of love and peace.

Preparing the pastor

Before all else, the pastor must prepare himself for the organization and the training program. There are three factors in the preparation. First, by prayer, Bible reading, and meditation the pastor will awaken the passion for souls within himself. He will seek the guidance of the Holy Spirit that his own life and administration may be fruitful. Second, he will study to familiarize himself with the methods and materials of visitation evangelism. He will decide how they are most applicable to his own church or churches. Third, he will experiment with these methods of securing decisions by making prospect calls himself before he asks his people to undertake them, even though he realizes that in most instances laymen are more effective in securing decisions than the average minister.

When the pastor has the inspiration in his own heart and is thoroughly familiar with the methods and materials, he is ready to organize his own program and to give the instruction talks. He should always remember that time is exceedingly important. No one of these talks should exceed thirty minutes. He must close on time, not one minute late!

The instruction talks

In the second section of this book are printed the instruction talks most necessary in training visitors in evangelistic calling. They are written as they have been given on many occasions in actual instruction to visitors. Many pastors will wish to take them exactly as they are printed. They contain all the essentials of the best visitation instruction. No minister need feel that he is plagiarizing by using them. They are already plagiarized. These instructions are not sermons in which a minister transmits truth through his own personality. Instead they are methods of practical procedure which have been worked out by many minds and under many differing experiences. They are in no sense the product of my own discoveries, although I have added some personal points and illustrations, as each minister will undoubtedly wish to do as he presents them to his people. Those personal elements make the instructions living and vital. But these materials have come from many sources and minds. They belong to the Christian ministry. So no one need hesitate to use them just as they are, as they suit his purpose.

Each minister may add, subtract, or revise these materials as occasions demand so as to make them adaptable to his own church and community. However, a word of warning. The method of procedure in visitation evangelism here presented is the refined experience of thousands of situations and innumerable evangelistic pastors and evangelistic directors. It is not wise to change them unless a pastor has proved his own ideas by wide experience, and even then for the first program he undertakes in visitation evangelism he had better use these to prove their truth!

When the minister has mastered these training instructions he is ready to organize his own campaign.

CHAPTER VI

Assimilating New Members

"UNLESS YOU GET A NEW MEMBER TO BECOME ACTIVE in the life of your church within thirty to sixty days after he joins, he will become a liability," said an experienced preacher to a group of theological students. "There are a few exceptions," he added. "But I maintain that my principal proposition is true. Quickly get them active or watch them become spiritual invalids or corpses."

Unless a convert or a newly transferred member begins by attending church and participating in the activities, and unless he becomes a regular contributor within two months, the chances are that he will become merely one of those numerous individuals whose only connection with the church is that his name is inscribed on its rolls and that he attends on Easter Sunday, if that happens to be convenient.

One of the most serious problems of American church life is the inactive church member. If it is anywhere near true that on any Sunday two thirds of the members are absent from the worship of God, and that less than one half are regular contributors, then something is seriously wrong with both our devotion and our methods. It is amazing how much the church accomplishes in spite of so many ineffective and spiritually crippled members. No military force and no other organization on earth could last very long with so great a casualty list.

Undoubtedly the world, the flesh, the devil, and

indifference have weakened or destroyed the churchmanship, not to mention the Christian effectiveness, of a great percentage of church members. But I believe that this inert body of church members is more like an unharnessed river, which if sufficient dams were erected and power plants built, would transform great lakes into spiritual power to be used in the church and out in the world. There is tremendous unused spiritual and moral power in our laity, ready to be released if the church is wise enough to recover it.

Perhaps the fault lies more with the church than with the new members. The Bible says that they are "babes in Christ." The church should not expect them to shift for themselves, even the newly adopted children. Nonparticipation of members can often be traced back to inadequate assimilation when they were new members. Many pastors are exceedingly anxious to win new converts but are not willing to give time and attention to their spiritual growth. Babies live only by nurture and careful diet, and youths become strong only by training and proper exercise. We should be as anxious to deepen these people in their religious life and to strengthen them in their church activities as we were to win them in the first place. We should help them to grow in the grace and likeness of Jesus Christ.

The following program is designed to reduce the casualties to a minimum and to hold in vigorous active Christian life those who have decided to follow the Master and to become his churchmen.

ASSIMILATING NEW MEMBERS

Attention before uniting with the church

Each decision in the home, whether a first commitment to Christ or a transfer of church membership, should be accompanied by a period of consecration. If at all possible this should be conducted by the visitors at the time the decision is made. If the visitors feel they cannot lead in such a dedication in prayer, then the pastor should follow up with a later visit before Membership Sunday.

It is of great importance for the pastor to have a pastoral instruction period with each family before they unite with the church. Some ministers do this by personal calls upon each family. Others set a week night for a period of thorough instruction and prayer with the group who are to unite on a particular Sunday. Some pastors use effectively a pastoral instruction conference for young people and adults similar to the pastor's instruction of children. Wherever it appears necessary, individual spiritual guidance should be given.

Both the lay visitors and the pastor should clearly indicate to new members that their decision involves a lifetime habit of regular attendance at church services in the public worship of God.

The nurture of the soul is in the corporate worship of God and in the fellowship with his people. Such weekly dedications along with private devotions mature into the largest public service.

Conversion into active members

If the first responsibility of the pastor and the church is to help light or relight candles of faith in these new people, then the second is to help them to become active members of the congregation. Experience proves that this integrating process must be accomplished in about thirty to sixty days. If a new member immediately starts to attend church regularly, to contribute, to take part in activities, then the possibility of his becoming a lax and unfaithful member is negligible.

Some definite methods need to be adopted to weld the spiritual interests to regular church habits and work. There are various effective ways used in different churches. The following program is presented because it enables the pastor to keep close touch with all his new members as well as to integrate them into the life of the church. It also places responsibility on present members in a fellowship with the new people who come into the church.

A friend for each new member

The week following the new member's reception into the church a visitor calls. The visitor tells the new member that he is glad of the decision and welcomes him into the congregation. During the conversation he tells about the church, its services, its youth meetings, its midweek service, its church school, and the work of the women. Whatever may appear to be of interest to the newcomer is discussed and explained. Particular importance is laid upon attendance at the worship of God. Church attendance as a life habit is stressed. The visitor concludes by saying that he expects to meet the new member at church next Sunday.

Then during the following month or two this visitor who has been appointed to sponsor the new member looks for him at church services, introduces him to members of the congregation, and sees that he is properly attached to the organizations of the church to which he is entitled. If the visitor does not see him at church services, he telephones or calls upon him. The visitor's duty is to see that the new member establishes the habit of church attendance during the month or so after he unites with the church. This is a very beautiful, kind, and thoughtful service, and the new member may soon discover that he is an integrated part of the church life. He may never know that this friend who called and who took such an interest in him was appointed to this high responsibility by the pastor.

Appointment of sponsors

The pastor must give a great deal of consideration to the selection of a sponsor. The sponsor should be above all a good Christian and a devoted churchman. No one should ever be assigned to a new member because it might help the old member to become more attentive to church duties. Only those should be chosen who the pastor is reasonably certain will carry out the responsibility, and whose own lives are surrendered to the will of the Master.

Very often an entire family unites with the church. Then a family should be appointed to sponsor them. For instance, Mr. and Mrs. John Randolph and their two children, a daughter of sixteen and a son of ten, united with the church on Sunday. Monday morning the pastor looked over the possible sponsors in the neighborhood. He discovered one of his officials, Frank Baker, who had a wife and two sons, one about ten and the other seventeen. The fact that the oldest boy was a little older than the Randolph girl would add the boy-and-girl interest, he thought.

On Wednesday the Bakers received a letter from their pastor asking them to sponsor their neighbors, the Randolphs. On Friday evening the Randolphs had company. At church the next Sunday the two families sat together. Sunday night Mary Randolph and Bill Baker came to the young people's meeting. And of course the two younger boys quickly became fast friends. The following week both women were together at the women's society.

The church and its life became the central influence with these two families, and it happened that several years later the minister officiated at the wedding of Bill and Mary, although he originally had no idea that Bill would take on the responsibility of being permanent sponsor to Mary.

In this instance, as whenever the pastor makes a wise selection, the sponsoring members assumed their Christian responsibility gladly.

Checking on the sponsors

It is necessary to check on the sponsor to be certain that he carries out his duties. A successful pastor once said, "Church administration is based on two essentials: first, the selection of the right layman to do the work; second, and more important, a check on that layman to see that he has done

ASSIMILATING NEW MEMBERS

it." It is necessary to confirm the willingness of a sponsor and to be certain he has not been negligent. Sometimes we learn this necessity by disappointing experience.

This problem of members who were becoming ineffective and unfaithful had long weighed upon my mind and spirit. So I devised a system of sponsors. I would write the sponsor and ask him to serve, expecting that he would do so without putting him on a leash. So far as I knew, it was working well enough, until one day one of the officers of my official board said, "What is the name of that new member you wanted me to go see? I intended to go at the time, but it slipped my mind. It must have been six months ago!"

Instead of feeling disappointed in my layman I realized that it was time for me as pastor to check up on myself, and to discover some method of finding out when the work had been done. If a man as faithful as this official could overlook this matter, what about those who were less devoted?

There are two methods of keeping account of the effectiveness of the sponsors. In our church we write a letter to the sponsor telling him he is appointed to serve and explaining what we expect him to do: visit in the home immediately, help the new member to get located in the church organizations, see that he is attending church services, and help him to get acquainted with the church people. A post card is enclosed, addressed to the pastor. The sponsor merely checks on the card the sentence: "( ) I have visited the new member." Then he signs his name and drops it in the mail. If the card is not returned within one week, the pastor calls the sponsor on the telephone.

The second method used by some pastors is to write a letter making the assignment and before the week is out to telephone the sponsor getting his agreement to serve. This is followed the next week by another telephone call asking for a report.

A work sheet

To keep a record of the progress of his new members, the pastor prepares a work sheet like the one illustrated on the oppposite page (Form E). Cardboard is better to handle than paper. The sheet is divided vertically into two sections. The first section contains the information about the new member. The second section records the information about the sponsor. Each horizontal line, therefore, gives the name of the new member and information about him and his sponsor. The vertical columns provide spaces opposite each name for recording the progressive accomplishments. Each card bears about twenty names of new members.

The first section, containing the information about the new member, is divided into vertical columns as follows: 1. Name, address, and telephone number. 2. Manner in which he united with the church (P—profession of faith; T—transfer of membership) and the date. 3. Date of visit from pastor or church assistant. 4. Organizations in which the member becomes affiliated. This is the essential information.

Some pastors wish to keep a more complete rec-

MEMBER ADDRESS PHONE	WHEN & HOW REC'D	PAST. LETTER	PAST. VISIT	QUEST. SENT	FIN. LETTER	PLEDGE REC'D	ORGANI-ZATIONS	SPONSOR ADDRESS PHONE	PAST. LETTER	REPLY	PHONE CALL

NEW MEMBERS AND SPONSORS

FORM E. NEW MEMBER AND SPONSOR RECORD

ord of the new members and their activities. In our church we add these columns: 5. A check mark indicating that a personal letter of welcome has been sent from the pastor. 6. A check mark indicating that a questionnaire has been sent requesting the new member to indicate his previous church activities, record of service, and willingness to work where assigned. 7. A check mark indicating a letter has been sent about ten days after membership concerning the financial program of the church. 8. The date when a pledge has been received.

The second section, containing the information about the sponsor, is divided into vertical columns as follows: 1. Name, address, and telephone number of the sponsor. 2. Date pastoral letter is sent notifying the sponsor of his assignment. 3. Date the reply card is returned. 4. Date a pastoral check-up telephone call is made.

The value of this work sheet is apparent. Here is the romance of the grace of God growing in the life of the new member. It is fascinating to see the development recorded. Also any failure to assimilate the new member becomes apparent before it is too late to do anything about it. On one work sheet the pastor, any member of the church staff, or any volunteer lay worker has before him at a glance the history of some twenty new members of the church. It shows immediately whether the new members are being assimilated into the church and, if not, where the deficiency lies.

This program of assimilation is not a mechanical one. Instead it uses the personal method emphasized by Jesus that his way of life is a matter of personal contagion. New members are won to Christ and to affiliation in a particular church by the personal invitation of some Christian men or women. They are received in personal relationship to their pastor. They are then assimilated into the congregation, becoming active members, through the responsibility of seasoned fellow members.

"Do they stick?"

A very logical and pertinent question is often raised, "It is apparent that this method of visiting in the homes will secure decisions. But are they sincere? Are spiritual commitments made? Are people's lives actually changed? Has the saving grace of Christ transformed them? And do they make faithful members of the church?" One minister put the question, "Do they stick?"

The best test of all is that applied by Jesus: "By their fruits ye shall know them."

By that test the answer is in the affirmative. Remembering that some seeds fall by the wayside, some fall on rocky soil, and some fall among thorns where neither God nor man can prevent their going astray, nevertheless, the percentage of those won through visitation evangelism who remain faithful is very high. Many careful surveys have been made by pastors in churches large and small and in all kinds of communities. The results are the same. After a year of membership those who have been won by personal solicitation have as high—or higher —permanence in the life of the church as those won by any other method. Remarkable fidelity is shown where an assimilation program has been carefully followed through. One pastor reported that of ninety-nine received into membership in a visitation program a check-up a year later showed that of those remaining in the community only one had fallen away.

In our church we made a survey by name of the 1,043 new members received during forty-five months. The majority of these were won by laymen in visitation in the homes. At the time of the compilation 785 remained as resident members, the rest having moved away. The following were the results: Thirty per cent of the present membership had united with the church in these forty-five months. Six hundred twenty, or 80 per cent, were identified *by name* in some organization of the church, church school, women's society, etc. Of the remainder some are known to be regular attendants at church services, but their number cannot be ascertained accurately. Of the contributors to the budget 37 per cent come from the 30 per cent of new members. Of the 133 officers in the church school 59, or 44 per cent, are new members. These include 36 superintendents or teachers, 23 officers, and 5 on the board of education. The "old" members have not been displaced. Instead, the participation by the new members has enabled us to enlarge our program twofold and to increase our effectiveness in the missionary work of the kingdom.

Each pastor who wins his new members by personal solicitation through his laymen can see in the

ASSIMILATING NEW MEMBERS

lives of his people that they are committed to Christ and are endeavoring to live the Christian life. The test of Jesus, "By their fruits ye shall know them," has been applied in hundred of churches, and the members won through personal invitation are not found wanting either in Christian living or in loyalty to the church.

PART II: THE INSTRUCTION OF THE VISITORS

---INTRODUCTION---

"FOR TO THIS END HAVE I APPEARED UNTO THEE, TO appoint thee a minister and a witness both of the things wherein thou hast seen me, and of the things wherein I will appear unto thee." (Acts 26:16.)

As Christian ministers we are ordained to reveal to others both the known experience of Christ and the possibilities yet to come. In our training conferences we are to present our understanding of how Christ works through people who have qualified themselves as his ambassadors and also to make them expectant of miracles of grace as men and women shall be born into the Kingdom.

The art of training people as visitors is founded upon two basic principles: first, upon certain accepted and proved procedure; second, upon interesting and fascinating presentation. The minister can conduct the instruction periods in such attractive form that people will be captivated by the thrilling challenge to this divine labor of love.

This section is devoted to the guidance of the pastor in giving the instructions to the visitors. The first division of each chapter provides the reasons for the particular instruction, including the objectives and the results to be expected. It explains the "why" of that particular instruction.

The last division is the actual instruction material itself. Each instruction covers a basic subject in its briefest and most understandable form. Each set of instructions should be given without omitting a sin-

INTRODUCTION TO PART II

gle point, for each point has been included to meet a fundamental question or an actual situation which the visitor will encounter.

As each pastor gains experience in giving these instructions, he may then wish to enlarge or shorten certain parts. In every instance the pastor will want to use illustrations which grow out of the visiting by his own people.

In the actual presentation to the visitors the pastor may use an outline or give the material from memory, but under no circumstance should the material be read. No sales manager ever reads instructions to salesmen. This material is not static, formal words. Instead it is living, vital reality. Spontaneity comes through unhampered presentation. A pastor needs to appreciate the meaning of each part of the instruction, to discover the reasons for its inclusion, and to present it to the visitors as living experience.

The reader will notice that in this section there is some repetition of materials previously covered. The reason is that the lay visitors need certain information concerning the entire project. They will have no opportunity to secure any information concerning the program other than that included in the actual instruction periods.

The key to success is promptness in beginning, succinctness in presentation.

―――――――――――CHAPTER VII―――――――――――

Securing the Decision

First Night's Instruction—Time: 6:35–7:05

THE TIME HAS ARRIVED FOR THE PASTOR TO BEGIN HIS first instruction period. Few of the visitors have ever participated in this type of visitation. Most of them are almost certain that they have undertaken something beyond their powers.

In a brief introduction the pastor points out to them that during the week two features of visitation evangelism are combined. First, they will be visiting in the homes of the people to win them to Christian discipleship and resident church membership. Second, and equally important, they will be attending a school of instruction. Every visitor must be present every session. Nothing should be allowed to keep anyone away. Promptness is urged. Be on time, six fifteen—or six o'clock, if possible—and the pastor will quit on time!

Let the laymen know that this method is scriptural, instituted by Jesus, practiced by Jesus in his interviews, and that any layman in this group *can* do this kind of work. Tell them that every team present will win at least one person before the week is out and some will secure many new members.

This first instruction explains to the visitors:

1. How to prepare for the call, including prospect cards and reports.

2. How to gain entrance into the home in a friendly way.

3. How to secure the decision for a transfer of membership to your church, including the excuses often met and how to answer them.

4. How to secure the decision of a person not professing to be a Christian, including the difficulties he faces and how to overcome them.

5. How to close the interview by securing a favorable decision.

6. How to conduct a spiritual commitment when the decision is made.

THE INSTRUCTION
SECURING THE DECISION

During this week we are combining two features in visitation evangelism. First, and exceedingly important, is our visiting in the homes of people whom we hope to win to Christ and to membership in our church. Second, and no less important, is our being together for a school of instruction each night.

We will meet at six fifteen—if you can make it, be here at six o'clock—conclude our supper by six thirty-five, and spend thirty minutes in instruction before going out to our visiting. We will end our sessions each evening promptly at seven five. You should be at the home of your first call by seven fifteen. When we end this discussion, don't stop for any conversation or visiting here at the church. Your business is to get to the first home immediately. Leave as quickly as you would if someone shouted, "Fire!"

Tonight we will discuss "Securing the Decision." Tomorrow night we will talk about "Efficient Visiting," Wednesday night "Difficult Cases," and Thursday night "Family Evangelism." You see from the varied subjects of these discussions that every visitor will need the entire course of instruction. Let nothing prevent your being present at every one of these meetings.

Following the meeting tonight you will go in teams of two with your list of prospects, and during the evening you may confidently expect that at least one third of you will win one or more families. Before the week is over you can feel assured that practically everyone here will have won at least one new member. Some of you will have secured a number of church memberships.

Promptness is essential in this program. The supper begins at six fifteen. If at all possible, be here ahead of that so that you can give me your report. Every report should be in my hands not later than six twenty-five.

Christ's method

The greatest service you can render to any person is to introduce him to Jesus Christ. Suppose that each team of laymen present tonight would secure the decision of some youth for Christian living so that in the coming years this youth would grow into fine Christian manhood. It would develop for him dependable character, the highest type of citizenship, a Christian home, Christian training for his children, and a life lived in the fellowship and service of God. Can you think of any greater thing you could do?

SECURING THE DECISION

Christ expects this service from us. He taught his disciples to become fishers of men. He introduced and sent out two by two both his twelve disciples and the seventy. He tells us, "Go ye ... and make disciples."

This method Christ used himself. In the Gospel of John are recorded fourteen personal interviews. There was the simple invitation of Jesus to Matthew, "Follow me." He interviewed Zacchaeus and the woman at the well. Christ won Andrew, and Andrew brought his brother Peter to Jesus. Philip met Jesus and hastened to Nathanael with the good news. Jesus won adults and took time to teach the twelve and the seventy how to do the same. When he was crucified, he left a group of trained men to work as he had worked—person to person. And thus the age-long process began.

Now by this very same method Jesus sends us out to seek disciples for him. And the interesting promise is that everyone of you will win at least one person during this week. Presumably half of the prospects called on tonight will be won. It is universal experience that laymen who do this work have the greatest joy of their lives. All you need to do to obtain results is to follow the brief and definite instructions, go out led by Christ's spirit, and do the best you can.

Quietly, above the confusion and heartbreaks of our day, Jesus is saying to us, "This is the way, walk ye in it. Ye must build in the midst of devastation. Ye must create while others destroy. Follow me!"

A WORKABLE PLAN OF EVANGELISM

> O teach me, Lord, that I may teach
> The precious things thou dost impart;
> And wing my words, that they may reach
> The hidden depths of many a heart.

Teams of two

You are to go in teams of two. You will receive six to eight assignments. The reason for this number is that some will not be at home. You should be able to make three or four calls this evening.

A friendly visit

First, read the information on the Prospect and Assignment Card. It will give you a lead as to why the prospect is on our responsibility list.

Then, before you reach your first home, decide whether you or your companion will lead in the conversation. The one not leading should come into the conversation only when absolutely necessary. At the second home you may change and let the other member of the team lead. Have a prayer in your heart for these people as you come to their home.

At the door, explain why you have come. It is a visit from your church. You may say, "Your children are in our church school and we have come for a friendly visit in the interest of religious instruction." You will receive a welcome to come in. Make your visit friendly, taking an interest in the children and in the home. Do not talk about the weather or politics. Mark Twain said, "More is said about the weather and less done about it than any other subject." Hold to your subject, Christ and membership in his church.

SECURING THE DECISION

Church transfers

Assume that your prospect is a member of a church somewhere and that you are to secure the transfer of his membership. Inquire about his church membership. Get all the facts you can. Suggest to him one or more reasons for making the transfer. He may make his decision immediately, although he probably will give you some excuse for not moving his membership. You must answer his excuse if it is presented, but do not let it dismay you. Rather let it be a challenge to your wisdom and understanding.

1. The excuse most often given is a *sentimental one*. He has ties with the old home church which he does not wish to break. Point out that if no one moved his membership there would be no church. Ninety per cent of the members of urban churches have transferred from some other congregation. Over half the members in the average rural community of America are transferred members. The church-school teachers who train his children have transferred to this church. Without transferred members there would be no church school. Then the individual who does not have a church home loses; his family loses; and the Kingdom in the world loses. We are not apt to serve unless we belong.

The most vital way in which we may honor and renew old ties of affection is through a continued and effective service to Christ. Loyalty to the past is of no value except as it translates itself into the present and the future. We must do more than look backward, however dear and precious those days were.

2. The second excuse usually given is: *"We do not know how long we shall be here."*

It is true, no one of us knows how long he will be here! We may get the great summons today or tomorrow. But it is easier to move a church membership than it is to move a trunk. It takes only a postage stamp, and the church will provide it. The pastor will be glad to send for your membership. The best way to find friends and to have roots in the community is to have your church home where you live. If you move away only six months from now, the pastor will send your church certificate to a church in your new community.

This is another case of procrastination with deadening results. Loss of contact with Christ's church means loss of interest. Loss of active participation is a stalemate on the road to Christian greatness. You have to be alive to the church and be a part of the church. F. W. Norwood said, "Life's greatest tragedy is to lose God and not to miss him." This can so easily happen when for one reason or another we postpone our allegiance to his cause.

Remind the prospect that procrastination is the most dangerous attitude possible. It is the cancer that is eating away the vitals of American church life. If every nonresident member would move his membership and become an active church member, the effectiveness of the church would be increased at least fifty per cent. He will strengthen the church as well as his own life by active participation.

3. Occasionally a person admits that *he does not want to assume any responsibility* for service. Per-

haps he carried too big a load in the old church, but to drop out altogether would seriously impair his Christian life.

Eventually such people expect to become active in the church, but for the time being they choose to sit on the sideline. The trouble about that is that it presents a critical danger, for in putting God off they may soon discover they have put him out. There is no such thing as neutrality with life. We never can take a vacation from our responsibilities. No one can be "out of pocket" in relationship to his church without the inevitable loss of Christian growth. Christ said, "He that is not with me is against me." Life is lived day by day. If it is not lived actively in accordance with God's purpose then, whether intentionally or not, it is lived by some other purpose and faith. There can be no postponement of responsibility. To refuse to make a decision is nonetheless a decision in itself.

The only way to increase our spiritual life is to give away our powers. These are days when the very structure of civilization is attacked from without and from within. No Christian can afford to relinquish his responsibility. You owe it to your family, your friends, your world, your Christ to use what strength, time, and talent you have in building his Kingdom.

4. Again some person may say that he *does not want to assume financial obligations*. The largest contribution is not money but a life. To occupy a pew every Sunday is of inestimable value. To live a Christian life in the church and out of it is a great

gift. If you sincerely cannot give money, give of your time and talent. When you are in a position to contribute, of course you will do so.

"For where your treasure is, there will your heart be also." This is a very real truth. We recognize that the income of some is uncertain, thus interfering in some ways with their church membership. Yet an abundance of wealth or security of income has no rightful place in influencing a decision for Christ. One of the loveliest New Testament stories is that of the widow who gave what she had out of her great devotion. Once our hearts are in the keeping of the Saviour a portion of our material substance, large or small, will find its way into the treasury. There is only one compelling surrender, and once that is offered other things take their rightful place.

> Take my heart, it is thine own;
> It shall be Thy royal throne.
> Take my love; my Lord, I pour
> At thy feet its treasure store.
> Take myself, and I will be
> Ever, only, all for thee.

About ninety per cent of the church transfer problems center around these four excuses. Answer them as best you can.

Securing the decision of nonmembers

If the person is not a member of any church, then assume that he has had some religious background and training in his youth. Nineteen out of twenty people upon whom we call have attended church or church school at one time or other. Assume also that he believes in God and in Jesus Christ. Finally, assume that since he has had some contact with your church he wants to become a Christian and a member of Christ's Kingdom and church.

Lead your prospect by affirmative suggestions. Never suggest the negative. Do not allow him to say, "No," or "Not now," if you can help it.

Your own personal experience in the Christian life, what Christ means to you or in your home, or to a friend, will aid tremendously in winning him.

Let us remember that we are *never* to ask him to attend church, or invite him to come because we have a fine pastor, or the choir sings well, or ours is a friendly church. He knows when we compromise. Hold steady for Christ and a Christian home. Ask him for a definite decision of loyalty to Jesus Christ and membership in the church.

If he gives an excuse or reason for a negative reply, it will probably be one of these three:

1. *He has sinned and cannot break with the past.*

This is the heart of the Christian gospel. Jesus said he came to save sinners. Everywhere in the Bible God forgives those who have sinned and wish to turn to the right. God enables people to break with the past. His power will cleanse anyone who trusts in him. He will give the strength to live the Christian life. Becoming a Christian is an act of faith. Repentance for sin and trust in God will clear the way for the new life.

2. *He is afraid he can't make good.*

Explain that the first step is an act of the will; after that God promises, "My grace is sufficient."

Point out the Christian resources of personal prayer life, religious worship, Christian study, and Christian service as sources of strength and guidance to help him make good.

A Christian layman went to a friend who through drink had lost his legal practice and almost his health, and whose wife and children had left him. He invited him to turn his life over to God and to become a Christian. The man replied, "I would give anything in the world if I could do that. But I would only be an embarrassment to the church. I have often promised God and my wife that I would never touch liquor again, but I can't keep my promise. I'd join the church tonight if I thought I could hold out, but I can't."

In the inspiration of that moment the layman replied, "You don't have to hold out. Your business is not to hold out but to hold on. If you hold on to God, he will enable you to hold out. You live only one moment at a time. In that moment, by God's help, you can resist your temptation, can't you? Well, you never live more than one moment at a time. You hold on to God, and he will take care of time and of eternity."

That lawyer gave his heart to God and has been holding on through prayer and consecrated living, with his family returned to him, and in a good legal practice for thirty years. God provides the grace for everyone who trusts him.

3. He will want *to put it off*—to procrastinate.

Appreciate the willingness of the prospect to think it over. But things we put off never get done. It is harder every time we put it off. No question is ever settled until it is settled right. And you will have to face it again and again unless you settle it now.

Technique of closing

Let me suggest a method of closing your interview. This is exceedingly important.

If at any time you feel that you are making no progress and that it is time to go, you can always conclude by rising, and saying, "We are glad we had this visit. Think it over. We hope you will make yours a favorable decision soon. And in the meantime, come visit our church." Then you may leave.

If you are ready to secure the commitment, take out the Record of Decision Card (Form F, page 115). On it are three choices:

1. A decision for the Christian life—to become a follower of Jesus Christ.

2. A decision to unite with the church and the willingness to present oneself on Membership Sunday (unless the pastor has some other method or time of receiving members).

3. A desire to transfer membership from a certain church to our church.

You have your Record of Decision Card in your hand. Check the decision to be made, and give the card with a pencil to the prospect. Ask him to read it and, if that meets his purpose, to record his decision.

While the Spirit of God is leading him, the card enables the prospect to bring visually into focus the question he has faced for some time. We are accustomed to learn more through sight than through hearing. Here he visualizes his decision. He is impelled to make it.

If he tries to return the card, avoid taking it. Let him look at it a few moments longer, while you give another reason why he should take the step you are suggesting.

Then if he continues to return the card, accept it, ask him to think it over, and tell him that he will receive another call later. Then pass on to your next home. An interview should last not more than twenty or thirty minutes.

Spiritual commitment

If your prospect has agreed, there should be a moment of spiritual consecration. Suggest that you pray. As you pray express gratitude to God for his blessings, for the commitment made, and for his grace in Christian growth.

If you cannot pray in the presence of others, then tell the prospect that the minister will call within the next two weeks to give him spiritual guidance.

Sending them forth

You have your Prospect and Assignment Cards. You have your teammate. Follow these instructions as best you can. God's Spirit is guiding you. Do not waste a moment, but go immediately to the first home, and return tomorrow night at six fifteen. Good night.

RECORD OF DECISION

I believe in Jesus Christ and purpose with his help to live a Christian life.

I desire to unite with the _____ Church, and plan to present myself for membership Sunday, _____

I wish to transfer my membership to this church. For letter write to _____ at _____

My name stands on record there as _____

Name _____

Address _____

FORM F. RECORD OF DECISION CARD

CHAPTER VIII

Efficient Visiting
Second Night's Instruction—Time: 6:35–7:05

THIS SECOND NIGHT'S INSTRUCTION IS PROBABLY THE most directly helpful of any of the series. It presents the technique of "Efficient Visiting."

The pastor first makes certain that his people understand that no technique, however efficient, is enough. "The Spirit himself beareth witness with our spirit." This is a divine commission. Also, unless a person has a real interest and concern for others, his techniques are merely instruments wielded by unwilling hands. Loving others as Christ has loved us must be the impelling motive.

But there are right and wrong ways of doing God's work. Each of us needs to be an effective, serviceable workman "that needeth not to be ashamed."

Out of thousands upon thousands of evangelistic visits comes the experience of visitors that there are nine points which make visiting fruitful. By checking themselves with this procedure visitors learn quickly why they are getting decisions. When they fail, they are often able to discover the particular weakness in their presentation.

The pastor has placed at the plate of each visitor a card listing the "Nine Points of Efficient Visiting" (Form G, on the opposite page). He asks each person to memorize them, and during future visits to recall and constantly practice them.

NINE POINTS OF EFFICIENT VISITING

1. Secure a favorable environment.
2. Have one conversation at a time.
3. Ask questions.
4. Avoid a "No."
5. Don't argue.
6. Get decision of first one ready.
7. Don't close too soon.
8. Close as soon as possible.
9. Do your best; don't get discouraged.

FORM G. NINE POINTS OF EFFICIENT VISITING

He then proceeds to emphasize and illustrate them so that each person will go out to put them into practice and continually check his visiting by these standards. If the visitors have true concern for people in their hearts, seek the guidance of the Holy Spirit, and follow these nine points, they will have the maximum of success.

Reports

Beginning on the second night and continuing each succeeding night, reports of the previous night's work are secured.

SUMMARY OF REPORTS OF VISITATION

Team	Persons Interviewed	First Decisions	Transfers	Total Decisions
Total Today				
Previous Total				
Total to Date				

FORM H. SUMMARY OF REPORTS OF VISITATION

EFFICIENT VISITING

These reports are gathered by the pastor himself while the visitors are at the supper tables. The pastor will not eat at the regular time but should do so either before or after the evening session. These are most important minutes for the pastor. He gathers the results of the previous evening's visiting, makes new assignments, and gives brief personal words of encouragement.

All prospect cards should be returned where homes have been visited. Upon the cards, on the face or back, should be written the favorable decision or the rejection and the reasons for rejection. Each team should sign the cards. No reports should be given orally. Decision cards should accompany favorable decisions.

A summary of reports should be compiled in a table (Form H, on the opposite page) to include:

1. The number of persons interviewed. (Count only the number of individuals who could have made a favorable decision. Do not count persons already members, members of other denominations, or people absent from home. Count only the individuals who were actual prospects.)

2. The number of first decisions (the individuals who have accepted Christ for the first time and who are to be received by profession of faith).

3. The number of transfers of memberships (the individuals who have decided to transfer their church memberships to the local church).

4. The total decisions.

Each night the pastor will add to the report of the preceding nights for the final totals. During the meal, the pastor will gather and tabulate the results so that he is ready to call the group to order for the reports at six twenty-five. Following the reading of the totals the pastor may give some such encouragement as this:

"Suppose that last night there had been revival services in our church and at the close of the sermon twelve persons came forward to unite with the church. We would have thought that that was a good beginning for special services, wouldn't we? Well, we had such a revival last night! Our visitors went out into the community preaching sermons of personal witness and testimony, and there is evidence that the Holy Spirit has guided them. Six of our teams secured twelve decisions. That means that one third of those calling secured the results the first night. There were seven first decisions and five transfers.

"If you did not secure a commitment last night, don't be discouraged. With the experience of last night and with further instruction more of you will secure decisions tonight, and certainly each of you will by the end of the week."

Then the pastor should call for a *very brief* report from one or more of the visitors who had success. Nothing will defeat defeat like success. A layman who tells of winning someone for Christ awakens in his unsuccessful neighbor the desire to go and do likewise. There is nothing comparable to the buoyancy of spirit that comes when a man realizes he is living creatively as a channel through which God's power enters human life. These personal reports,

EFFICIENT VISITING

even though sometimes haltingly told, are exceedingly helpful. But they must be concluded by six thirty-five.

Allow no one to tell of failure. If he had trouble or failure, let him discuss it with the pastor. Reports from successful callers should be given each night.

New assignments

Each night the pastor gives to every team new assignments of prospects in the neighborhood where they are calling so that the team goes out each night with six to eight prospective families.

THE INSTRUCTION
EFFICIENT VISITING

This evening we shall discuss the technique of "Efficient Visiting."

Let me again urge you to be present without exception the two remaining nights, because each discussion will be entirely different and highly valuable. Tomorrow night we will discuss "Difficult Cases," and will consider some of the issues that may have frustrated you. And the last evening we will conclude with a discussion of "Family Evangelism."

Let us preface the remarks concerning an efficient technique by again saying that technique is not enough. Our methods must be undergirded by a real interest in people, by prayer, and by Christ's spirit.

In the city of Louisville two men were visiting a man whom one of them knew very well. When it came to making a decision, it seemed as though he was going to say, "No," until his friend said, "In all the years that I have known you there is no man whom I have wanted to see become a professed Christian more than you. You have a Christian wife, and we need you in the church." There was a note of genuine warmth and love in his voice. The spirit tugged at the prospect's heart, and he gave his consent.

All the people whom we seek are the children of our heavenly Father; they are our brothers. Let us go in the sincere spirit of true concern for their welfare.

There are nine points to efficient visiting. If you follow these nine points, you will have the largest success. Checking yourself by them will help you to avoid making the same mistake a second time. One man came back to report on the third night of one campaign and said, "I lost a man last night. But I know what I did wrong. I missed on the fourth point. I let him say No at the beginning, and then I couldn't change him. I won't do that again."

1. Secure a favorable environment

The first point is, "Secure a favorable environment." As you enter a home, be in silent prayer. The home itself is the most favorable environment for a visit in the interest of the Christian life and the Christian family. Your prospect is your host. Establish a friendly atmosphere as soon as possible. Be interested in the home and its members.

But sometimes there are distractions. If there are visitors, it is best to excuse yourself. However, this is not always true. Use your judgment. Two men were calling in one home and found another man and his wife visiting the pospects. As they came in and the introductions were made, the two men felt they should leave. But before they could say anything, the visiting wife spoke up, "Oh, you are from St Mark's Church. I know, you have come to get Mr. and Mrs. Ballard to transfer their memberships. Well, my husband and I have just moved here. We ought to have our memberships transferred too." Within a few moments these men had secured the decision of both families, the husband in the home they were visiting making his first Christian profession.

If there are distractions, try to remove them. If the environment is unfavorable, create a situation where you and your prospects can give attention to Christian discipleship.

A blaring radio is often a "noisome pestilence." You can't very easily win a man to Christ to the syncopation of the latest popular tune. But there are two ways you may stop the radio. First, talk so low that your prospect will have to turn the radio off in order to hear you. Second, in case that is not effective, tactfully ask, "Would you mind if I lowered the radio?" Then lower it until it is silent!

2. Have one conversation at a time

The second principle is "Have *one* conversation at a time." Remember, before you enter a home you should decide whether you or your partner is to make the approach. Then do not set up a second con-

A WORKABLE PLAN OF EVANGELISM

versation. It causes static. If your partner is leading in the interview and someone else in the family tries to talk to you, give a courteous Yes or No and turn to the conversation your partner is conducting. Do not let your conversation go further. There is only the one matter of importance, the principal conversation regarding church relationship.

If you feel some point of emphasis, question, or instance would help toward the decision, feel free to make it and then leave the interview again in the hands of your partner.

3. Ask questions

Then ask questions. It is good salesmanship psychology to let the prospect take over the conversation. Don't monopolize it yourself. Talk just enough so that you will help direct your prospect to his own conclusion. Ask your questions progressively, starting with generalizations to which the prospect agrees, and then finally come to the leading question.

4. Avoid a No

Create a favorable Yes psychology. Ask only questions with which the prospect can agree. Do not ask a direct question to which he can answer No.

For instance, if you open your conversation by asking, "Wouldn't you like to join our church?" and the prospect replies, "No," then immediately you have lost your case. No one of us likes to change his position, once he has asserted himself, even if he finds himself to be wrong. Few people will reverse a negative reply, especially in the presence of strangers.

Perhaps a better approach would be, "You have your children in our Sunday school. You believe in the ideals and principles for which Christ and the Church stand. Don't you think your membership in the church would help your children in their Christian education?" The prospect can't say No to that. The worst he can do is to give you an excuse, which you can then proceed to answer. But you have not received a flat negative. Avoid a No.

5. Don't argue

Don't argue. You cannot argue anyone into the Kingdom of God. Whenever it is possible to agree with your prospect, do so. If he says, "There are hypocrites in the church," you can readily agree. You probably will not want to say, as Sam Jones once did to a similar inquiry, "Yes, and there is always room for one more!" You will probably reply in some such fashion, "Yes, unfortunately there are hypocrites in the church. There are in every worthwhile institution and in every country people who do not act loyally and faithfully. But that is no excuse for the rest of us. Judas was one of Jesus' disciples, but the other eleven finally proved faithful."

You will find many differences of opinion. If at all possible, agree with your prospect. Don't argue on matters which are not truly essential.

However, there are some subjects on which you cannot agree with a person—that is, in those conceptions of essential faith. If some man were to say, "Jesus Christ is merely a man like any other man, except perhaps the best of us," you could not let that go unchallenged. Jesus Christ is man, yes; but Jesus Christ is God, and our Saviour.

But avoid argument, if at all possible.

Now let me illustrate these last three points. They are, you remember, "Ask questions," "Avoid a No," and "Don't argue."

Two men went out together. One was inexperienced, and the other was a trained salesman. In this interview the inexperienced man led in the conversation, and almost immediately he said, "We should like to see you become a Christian and unite with our church." To which the prospect courteously replied that he appreciated their interest but would not do so then.

The salesman reported the following night, "I knew that we were sunk. Such a flat rejection practically ended the matter. But I thought I would try." Then he went on to say:

"I asked the man, 'Did you attend Sunday school in your youth?' and he replied, 'Yes, I went regularly until my middle teens, then dropped out.'

" 'Then you believe in God and in Jesus Christ?' I asked.

" 'Oh, yes,' he replied, 'I suppose everyone does when he thinks it through.'

" 'Your parents were Christian people, I gather?'

" 'Yes, they were very faithful. I wouldn't take anything for their Christian lives. And I'm glad they took me to Sunday school as a child.'

" 'Since you send your children to Sunday school, you evidently still believe in the church and the things for which it stands.'

" 'I certainly do. I wouldn't want my children reared in a community without a church. You couldn't get along without the moral sanctions the church teaches.'

" 'Don't you think it would be helpful to your children if you gave them the same advantage of a father who is a churchman as your parents gave you?'

" 'Yes, of course that would help,' he replied.

" 'If you took your place as a Christian man, don't you think it would help lead your family into the Christian life?'

" 'Yes, I'm sure that is right.'

" 'Now that you have given it further consideration and there seems to be no reason why you couldn't take this stand, won't you do this in the interest of your family?'

" 'Yes, I believe I'll change my mind and do it.' "

This prospect was led step by step into a favorable decision when he was given time to reach valid conclusions. At no place did the salesman give him a chance for a rejection until the end. To each question there was no possibility of a negative reply. The appeal was progressive. He broke down the general confession into several lesser but important decisions. The visitor avoided a No, led his prospect by asking questions, and did not need to argue.

6. Get decision of first one ready

Secure the decision of the first one in the family who is ready to make it. Then proceed to the next one evidencing the most interest. Sometimes a child will lead them. Again, the mother may be very willing to transfer her letter. Get her willingness definitely stated. On occasions the father is the most interested. When you find any member of the family is ready, then get his definite Yes. On the basis of that decision you can more readily secure the other members of the family who are more difficult.

7. Don't close too soon

Don't press for a decision too soon. You see, it is the decision of the prospect which must be made, and not your own. Let him talk about his excuses, answering them as best you can. Direct the conversation, but let him follow through until he honestly decides that he should become a Christian and unite with the church, or that he should transfer to our congregation.

8. Close as soon as possible

But, whenever the prospect is ready to decide, take that decision then and there on whatever basis the prospect wishes to make it. There may be many other advantages to the Christian life and to your church which you want him to know about. But those can come later. Don't oversell your proposition.

Haven't you had some salesman want to sell you a book or an electric sweeper which you wanted to buy, then keep on telling you how much better it was than a competing article, and go on and on until finally you wanted only one thing—to get rid of that salesman?

Your prospect has a definite decision to make. Whenever he is satisfied that it is right between him and God, you accept that decision. He has the rest of his life to learn more about Christ and Christian churchmanship. Remember if you get him started, God will help him to "become."

9. Do your best; don't get discouraged

And the final point: Do your best, and don't get discouraged. About a third of you have already secured at least one decision. It is possible the rest of you may win some tonight. If you see that you cannot close a case favorably, then do not close it. Leave it open. Ask your prospect to think about the matter, to pray about it. Then invite him to attend church. Tell him that you or someone else will see him again.

Don't be discouraged. One team in a certain church had gone two nights without a favorable answer. They felt the pastor should not have selected them. They were never meant for this kind of work anyway. But as they thought it over they renewed their faith that perhaps God could use them. On the third night the way opened for them; they secured favorable answers from three families with a total of eleven new members. Discouragement was turned into great joy.

Do not feel your efforts are wasted even though you see no results. In another church one team had no results by the third night. In fact they went all week with no decisions. But on the last night they thought they had one family. They had followed the instructions carefully. They established a friendly environment. One of them led in the conversation, satisfactorily answering the excuses, and directed the young couple to a decision of faith in Jesus Christ and a willingness to unite with the church on profession of faith on Membership Sunday.

Then the young husband said, "No! I don't think we will do it, not just now anyway." There was no further explanation, and the team left, discouraged and ready to quit.

But that wasn't the end of the story. Four weeks later at the close of a Sunday morning service this young husband and wife came forward and brought with them two other couples. All six of them united with the church on profession of faith.

And this is what had happened. On the night the visitors had come the young husband and wife had made their decisions. Then he had thought of these two couples who were their closest friends. They visited in each other's homes. They were constantly together. And he had thought to himself, "We do everything else together; it would not be right for us to enter this new life without our friends." The real Christian spirit of wanting to share the Christian life had caught hold of him. So he had told the visitors he wouldn't act then, but he had not told them the reason. They had gone away discouraged while he and his wife were going out to win the other two couples.

You can never tell how much good the Holy Spirit may do through your efforts. You plant, and God gives the increase, thirty-, sixty-, even a hundredfold. Only eternity will reveal what good you do this week.

Do the best you can, and don't be discouraged!

CHAPTER IX

Difficult Cases

Third Night's Instruction—Time 6:35–7:05

The visitors will encounter some situations on the first and second nights where they will be completely at a loss as to what to say. They will not know how to meet the argument or problems encountered. It would be better if they had the information of this instruction period on the first night, but since difficult cases are not ordinarily met, and some visitors use ingenuity enough to overcome them anyhow, the information in the first two instruction periods must precede this. The third night is the earliest possible point when this discussion can profitably come.

If a team of visitors meet a difficult situation and raise a question on the first or second evening, ask them to hold that question until the discussion on "Difficult Cases." Or the pastor may discuss the problem with them privately.

The purpose of this period is to familarize the visitors with the difficulties most frequently encountered, and to show them how to overcome and answer the objections raised.

The instruction material contains ten situations that present serious difficulties which sooner or later each team is likely to encounter. The time of the instruction period is not long enough to discuss all of them, so the pastor will need to decide on some five or six which he feels are most often met in his own community. In most American communities the discussion concerning Catholic-Protestant marriage is invaluable. In other communities the problem would never be met because there are no Catholics living there.

The pastor should decide which of these difficult cases he will discuss and present them in the manner suggested.

New assignments and reassignments

Each day the pastor will carefully go over each card showing a rejection. Some of the cards will be placed in his "Postponed File"; others will go into the "Dead File." There will be others whom the visitors may indicate, or the pastor may feel, need another call before the campaign is over. On the third and fourth nights the pastor will assign these "recalls" to new visitors, probably to those showing the best results. Some of these can be called upon again by the orignal team with splendid results after the instruction on "Difficult Cases."

THE INSTRUCTION
DIFFICULT CASES

We never know what we are going to run into in an interview. A variety of attitudes will be discovered. We need to know what we shall meet and how to handle the situation as effectively as possible. The greatest factor is common sense and good judgment. Tonight we will discuss these difficult cases.

There are three types of problem attitudes:

1. *Sincere obstacles.*—These are barriers, either real or imaginary, which stand between a prospect

and the decision he should make. The person wishes to make a favorable decision if only the barrier can be removed.

2. *Alibis and excuses.*—The prospect knows what he ought to do but does not intend to follow such a course. He therefore makes an excuse, rationalizes by showing that his negative course of action is really all right. The visitor must get behind the excuse or alibi to the real desire of the prospect and then in a friendly way show him that his position is only an excuse or alibi.

3. *Closed-mind attitudes.*—These are the most difficult of all problem attitudes to deal with. A mind set against a favorable decision cannot be changed unless the prospect is willing to think with us and honestly and fairly face his relationship to Christ and his responsibility to himself, his family, his friends, and the community.

Try to classify in your mind whether the problem of the prospect is a sincere obstacle, an alibi or excuse, or a closed-mind attitude. It will help you in your approach and conversation.

We shall discuss several of these difficult cases and suggested solutions.

Catholic-Protestant marriage

One of the most common problems is a Catholic-Protestant mixed marriage. Many times we feel that since one member of the family is a Catholic we Protestants should leave him alone. Instead we may be the only ones who can give assistance.

First, inquire if they were married by a priest.

If so, encourage the Catholic to be faithful in his religion, which he probably will be. Then urge the Protestant to be as faithful in attendance and prayer as the Catholic. We shall certainly not try to proselyte the Catholic.

If they were not married by a priest, they are unchurched. The Catholic Church does not recognize their marriage; their children are not being brought up under its teachings; and the Catholic is outside his church. We know at once that this is an unchurched situation and that if this family is to have a right relationship with Christ and religious training for the children it will have to be in a Protestant church. The Catholic knows quite well that he has severed his relationship with the Catholic Church.

Point out to the Catholic that there are three things Protestants and Catholics have in common: We worship the same God, our Father, revealed by Jesus Christ, our common Lord and Saviour. We repeat the same prayer, the Lord's Prayer. We use the same creed, the Apostles' Creed (in the denominations where this latter is used). These matters of form and worship are important to the Catholic.

There are several differences. In the Catholic Church a communicant confesses his sins to the priest, and finds peace and forgiveness through the authority of the church; but in a Protestant church the members make their confessions directly to God in prayer and receive through their personal communion a sense of forgiveness and peace. Confession through the priest is necessary in Catholicism. Conference with the Protestant minister is welcome and most helpful. In the Catholic Church only that scripture may be read by the laity which is designated by the church. In Protestantism the individual Christian selects whatever portion of the Bible he wishes to read; particularly for his guidance there are the four Gospels.

The similarity of basic belief makes adjustment possible, and the prospect will find a welcome and a church home.

The Catholic realizes the value of religious instruction, so you can say, "If you come into our Protestant church with your husband (or wife), then the children can be baptized, receive religious instruction, and at the proper time be received into the church. Thus you will unify your family in these sacred privileges."

Experience shows that one third of these mixed-marriage prospects can be won on the first visit and subsequently proper approach can win another third.

Most parents cannot resist the spiritual appeal of their children when they are helped to realize it. And usually they are most eager to co-operate with whatever will lend harmony and beauty to their home life. A good father is a man at his best. Therefore in appealing for a oneness in the family's religious adherence, the needs of the children are a substantial basis of approach.

Good enough outside the church

How shall we deal with the person who says, "I can be as good outside the church as inside. I live a Christian life without the help of the church"?

Ask the prospect through what channels came his high ideals and principles of life. Are they not basically Christian, handed down to him through the Christian Church? The power that makes him a good man outside the church is not self-generated; it is a spirit that comes from within the church. Then lead him to see that the hope of the future is not in individuals, no matter how good or unselfish they may be. The real problem is to make the teachings of Jesus the dominant guide in the individual and social life of the world. Only the organized church can carry on such a program.

Show him that the strength and influence of his life can be made much more effective if he combines them with the strength and influence of others. No army could gain a victory as individual soldiers, no matter how great their courage and determination.

> Like a mighty army
> Moves the church of God—

for the healing of the nations rather than their destruction. Urge him to become a part of a service enhanced by corporate effort.

The moral man

Probably the most widely heard excuse is, "There are hypocrites in the church. I am as good as most people I see going to church."

To which you may reply, "Yes, unfortunately there are people in the church as there are people in every organization who do not measure up to the standard. But if we took that attitude, requiring perfection in all who belong to an organization, we should have no lodges, no clubs, no public school system, and not even a government. There are people in all these who are fifth columnists and do not believe in the organization to which they belong, except for what they can get out of it." However, we must remember that while the church has many critics, it has no rivals.

Remind such a person that it is just because the church does have such high standards that we notice the imperfections in some of those who fail to reach its goals. Remind him that one of the functions of the church is to be a hospital to heal sick souls.

As important as is the Christian religion in these trying days, it is urgent that every person who would see the high ideals maintained should unite with other Christians in similar endeavor. Let us remember that the church has always been the whitest institution in any period of history!

The divided family

There are families where the denominational memberships are not the same and where they have not united with either church in the community. There are families where husband and wife will not join either denomination because they have two denominational loyalties.

1. If they are sincerely convinced of their denominational doctrines, then advise them to become active members of the two churches, and to do so at once.

In one of these campaigns a family was discovered who had been married over ten years and had never attended any church, except very occasionally, because he was a Baptist and she a Lutheran and neither would give in to the other. They were urged to become affiliated with both churches, and they did. Two years later they were found to be active and happy in their church life, the son attending with his father and the two daughters attending with the mother.

2. Except where denominational loyalty is a matter of essential belief, it is far better for the family to decide on one denomination. Religious differences sometimes become decisive so that the harmony of a home is broken. "A house divided against itself shall not stand." To bring the family together in the same congregation where they can train their children and be loyal Christians is to render that family a distinct service. Parents can keep two denominational loyalties alive, remaining faithful to their church responsibilities, but it is exceedingly difficult for the children. Advise them for their children's sake to make up their minds now and to put their church memberships together in some church. Use the interest of the children, and let them help you to get a definite decision from the parents.

Waiting for someone else

How shall we deal with the person who is waiting for wife or husband to unite with the church before making a decision?

When either partner in the home cannot be won,

it is usually better for the other not to wait. Waiting does no good. Appeal to the one who is ready. Suggest, "You come into the church now. Get the family started. Your action will make it easier for the others to follow." At least we will have one parent who will help in the religious training of the children. Very often the other will not stand in the way or object even though he may not co-operate for a time. Experience has shown that one who comes ahead often wins the other. But one who waits seldom if ever accomplishes his end. Rarely do we lift people to higher levels of Christian living by going down to their level. We lift them by bringing them up to ours.

People with hurt feelings

Frequently we come upon people who have been offended in the church, sometimes in earlier life, sometimes in another place, either by ministers or by other members of the church. These offenses may be real but are often imaginary.

This problem attitude can be dealt with best by giving the prospect the opportunity to talk himself out. This relieves the inner pressure and usually shows him how weak his case really is. If it appears genuine, we may acknowledge that a mistake has been made. But, after all, no one can allow his whole life to be colored and diverted from its true course by someone else's blunder. Ask him if he does not think it is to the best interest of his own religious life, his family, and his example in the community to let by-gones be by-gones. Point out that Christ and his kingdom need him as well as he needs to be in the Christian fellowship of the church.

The person who is not good enough

Occasionally we come across the person who feels that he is not good enough, that he cannot become a Christian and unite with the church until he has reached perfection.

Point out to him that this is the very reason for the church. We come not attesting our perfection. We come to Christ professing our weakness, our sin, our need. We "all have sinned, and come short of the glory of God." "Him that cometh to me I will in no wise cast out." "Christ came not to call the righteous, but sinners to repentance." We come to Christ just as we are. We then begin the Christian life, growing in grace and Christian character. Show the prospect that the Christian life is an unending growth and development in Christlikeness, and that no man wins the race until he first begins. If he begins, by Christ's help he can win. The resources of divine strength are sufficient for any man's need.

Parents who send their children

Parents who have had religious background often will be satisfied to say, "I send my children to Sunday school. I don't need to go to church any more."

One woman replied to such an excuse, "You send your children to church school because you want to provide them with a spiritual environment and because you know how barren your life would be without its early church training. And yet there is a serious void in your home of today that was not true of your childhood home. It is the *example*. Christianity is not a code of living. It is a life spent in relationship with Christ. Your children will be more powerfully influenced by your example than by their frequent or infrequent contacts with the church. Most active Christians come from a background of religious parents and Christian home life. To see Christ living in you will be your children's greatest inspiration.''

The person who does not know enough

Sometimes we meet a prospect who is attracted to Christ and the Christian life but who genuinely and sincerely feels that he doesn't understand everything he should. He may have tried to read his Bible, without proper guidance, and become more confused than enlightened. It may be that specific points cannot logically be acceped.

This type of prospect is often a keen thinker. He may be a scientific man. We must agree with him that there are certain things in the eternal verities of God that none of us understand, that finite mind cannot hope to exhaust infinity. Nor do we have to be able to accept everything, even the perplexing problems of scripture, in order to become Christian. Point to the fundamental fact that a Christian is a follower of Christ, one who is committed to serve him in the building of his Kingdom. Suggest to him that he does understand enough to throw the strength of his character and the influence of his life into the creation of a better world.

The person who does not like the minister

Again we come upon the individual whose chief objection is that he does not like the minister or that he does not like the reception he has had by the members of the church. We need to show such a person that there is something far more important than his individual relationship to any one individual, minister or layman, in the church. We are followers of Christ, not of Paul or Apollos or Cephas. We should not allow personal dislikes to keep us out of the fellowship of the church of Jesus Christ. It is our duty to give the influence of our lives to the building of God's order on earth, sometimes in spite of what other people do.

The person who is too tired to go to church

One of the chief alibis we meet is, "I do not want to unite with the church because I want to rest on Sunday morning." This very evidently is not a reason; it is just an excuse. This prospect would get up for anything that he thought was worth while or valuable to his life.

Try to show him there is a supreme need in every human soul. It is fellowship with the Divine. Sunday is a day of rest, but rest is more than physical relaxation. It is spiritual re-creation. There is no real rest or peace except as it comes through communion with the Father. There is nothing that can build up the nerves and energies worn down by the frictions of the week like the worship of God. "My grace is sufficient for thee." Relaxation is never as complete as when man draws upon spiritual resources. "They that wait upon the Lord shall renew their strength." When Oliver Wendell Homes was asked why he went to church, he replied, "I find that I have within me a plant called a soul, that needs watering at least once a week."

Hard places made smooth

An intelligent and sympathetic facing of the difficulties which prospects face often smooths the road and "clears a free way for the feet of God."

In a truly humble and sincere Christian spirit meet the obstacles as best you can, depending upon God to guide you. If you can help the prospects to come to sincere convictions concerning their relations to God and his church, they will bless the day you came into their home.

Edgar A. Guest, whose books have sold more than a million copies, is a Christian and a church member because he believes in it. He says: "So I attend church when I can, and do for the church what I can, because I believe in it. . . . It is my source of inspiration and strength and comfort, and I should be an ingrate and a fool to desert it now. Criticized and derided and belittled, ridiculed and mocked, as it is, the church still stands for all that is finest in our thought. It is still the mother of our greatest sons and daughters." (*Why I Go to Church*.)

CHAPTER X

Family Visiting and the Continuation Program
Fourth Night's Instruction—Time: 6:25–7:05

NOTE THE CHANGE OF TIME IN THE FINAL EVENING. THE instruction should begin at six twenty-five with a brief summary of the first three nights of calling. All visitors should be requested to return to the church (or parsonage) at nine thirty for a final tabulation of results. If some individual has an unusual report, ask him to tell it briefly. But place the emphasis on what all have accomplished together.

Projecting the continuation program

This is the opportune moment to lift this movement from a sudden burst of effective interest up to a high plane of sustained evangelism. It should now become a regular month-by-month program for continuous enlistment of new members.

The pastor calls attention to the results. They are so much more than had been expected. He capitalizes on the first response of the laymen. Just as the seventy returned to Jesus, so these laymen return full of joy. Practically every team will have won at least one person. Many of them will never have had such confirmation of their own spiritual life as during this week.

Ask the group if they feel the effort has been worth while. Almost unanimously they will agree. Then ask them if they think this kind of work ought to stop. They will probably express themselves like

FAMILY VISITING AND THE CONTINUATION PROGRAM

one layman who said, "Pastor, this ought to be just the beginning." They will feel that the work should continue. Tell them that many prospects were not interviewed because of lack of time and that new prospects will constantly be appearing. Then tell them that there is a method by which it can be carried on, although not as intensely nor with so much demand upon them.

Describe briefly to them the plan which you wish to adopt. You may choose to meet once a month, or to have a "Fishermen's Club," or a weekly luncheon of "Men Evangelists for Christ." Or you may plan for visiting in connection with the coming revival or a visitation during Lent. As pastor you will select the plan or plans which fit your church and community most satisfactorily.

You will then ask these visitors to volunteer to participate in the program briefly outlined, that the prayer of Jesus may be answered—that there be laborers enough for the ever-increasing harvest. Ask those who will continue in the work to raise their hands. Get their names as the basis for your future evangelism.

Family visiting

The second and larger portion of this instruction period deals with "Family Visiting," emphasizing the necessity of winning people in family groups. Experience has proved that it is easier to win a family than an individual.

The entire family are to be called together for the interview. The children should be present when the parents are approached. It is time for encouragement in family religion, and religious practices in the home.

The instruction should indicate how to win children and youth to Christian discipleship. It should show how to win parents through presenting the responsibilities of parenthood. The basis of appeal will be companionship of the entire family—father, mother, children, and young people—in the Christian life and in active church associations.

THE INSTRUCTION
I. THE CONTINUATION PROGRAM

I am certain that all of you are anxious to know the results of our visiting. I cannot give them to you because there is no way of tabulating spiritual achievements any more than there are any scales which can weigh love. A single decision for Christ outweighs all the effort we have made these few evenings. There is no method of evaluating the joy you have felt as you have seen people redeemed and dedicated. Some of you have had spiritual experiences this week which have been mountain peaks of glorious and transfiguring radiance. No one can ever sum up all the good which has been done in this program. We leave that to God and his future.

But here are the tabulated results, which of course do not include what we shall do tonight. In the three nights of visiting we have had _____ teams, who have interviewed _____ persons. There have been _____ first decisions, _____ transfers of membership, for a total of _____ new members for our

FAMILY VISITING AND THE CONTINUATION PROGRAM

church. After your calling tonight please report here at the church (or parsonage) at nine thirty for the final tabulation.

Now I want to raise a serious question with you. Are you satisfied to let this work stop with tonight? If we do let it drop, the most valuable part of our program will be lost. Many of our prospects were not interviewed because they were not at home. Some whom we did see need to be called on again, some even suggesting that we come back at a later date. And then we will be constantly finding new prospects from month to month. Do you feel that we should let them go by default, or do you feel like one layman in another church who said to his pastor, "Pastor, this ought to be just the beginning."

If this program could be carried on just as effectively, would you be willing to give one night a month to it? All it will take is just this one night each month.

Those of you who will continue this work and this joy of reaching others may indicate your willingness to be a part of our permanent organization. By your help we will see to it that every person in our community who is our responsibility shall, under God, be given an opportunity to become active in Christ's Church. If you will help, raise your hand. (Secure the names of those who volunteer and state when you will have your next meeting.)

II. FAMILY VISITING

In our closing moments let us turn to a consideration of "Family Religion."

A WORKABLE PLAN OF EVANGELISM

Let me point out what appears to be a contradiction in facts. While only about half of the people in the United States are church members, yet about nineteen out of twenty persons whom we visit have attended Sunday school or church sometime during their lifetime. Out of such a large number whom the church has touched more people ought to be church members. It is evident that somewhere there has been inefficiency in the religious education program of the past. The first responsibility of the church school is to lead boys and girls, men and women, to an allegiance to Jesus Christ and into membership in the Christian Church. Evidently with many of these the church school has not succeeded.

In Detroit an industrialist of international reputation was approached for church membership. He refused by saying, "I attended Sunday school as a boy, but no one took any particular interest in me. No one ever thought it important enough to talk to a mere boy about joining the church. Now that I am prominent the church seems to think it is important. They weren't interested in me as a boy. I'm not interested in the church now." Whether that man's attitude was correct or not, both he and his influence were lost to the church.

This is not an isolated instance. Therefore let us not permit a single boy or girl to slip through our fingers either because we are not interested or because we do not know how to approach youth attractively. The church school deserves a great deal of credit because it has been the principal feeder for church membership. While with many it has done only a partial work, that provides the foundation upon which we may now build for decisions in the Christian life. The most fruitful field for evangelism is with children and youth in the church school and with unchurched parents of such children. No person is more welcome in the home than the teacher of one's children.

The church school and its affiliated parents are the best evangelistic field; and those to win them are the church-school teachers and you who are trained visitors. We should never be satisfied until everyone has been presented in person with the claims of Christ upon his life and home. This past year one church reported, "We reached the 'perfect state' in our intermediate department. The superintendent stated that every parent and youth in the department had united with the church." Facetiously she added, "The only problem remaining with them is their growth into perfect Christian character!"

Interviewing the parents

You may be asking, "What are the best methods in family evangelism?" They follow the same principles which we have discussed but with special application to the family group. It is easier to win an entire family than a single individual because of the solidarity of the family. They have common interests and will usually do things for the best interest of each other.

When discussing church membership with parents you have powerful influences which the home brings to bear upon them. Because they are parents they know they cannot evade parental responsibilies. They realize this. As you point out the various reasons for the step, these parents emphasize them from their own personal experience. You suggest to them:

1. *Religious training of the child is needed in the home.* The church school has the children such a little time. The home has them several hours daily. The words which the teachers briefly impart are enhanced and animated by the precept and example of the parents, or they are obliterated by the conduct of the parents. What the parents are, the children will become. They make it easy or difficult for their children in Christian living.

2. *Their interest is in the child and his best development.* They live primarily not for themselves but for their children. There is nothing so important to the child's future as his moral and spiritual integrity. What shall it profit a parent to give everything else to a child and stand idly by while he loses his soul. To live in such a dangerous and tempting age requires Christian stamina, a life held fast by a supreme devotion to the person of Christ and his way on earth. The best interests of the child requires Christian parental guidance.

3. *Right attitudes are established very young.* The most permanent attitudes are established in earliest childhood, even before a child knows what is taking place. As a mother leans over the tiny baby, closes her eyes, and prays, the infant assumes an attitude of quietness, even though it understands not a word that is softly spoken. No one can begin

to estimate the importance of grace at the table, bedtime prayers, and the moments a mother sets apart to talk to her children about Jesus.

4. *They send their children to the church school.* They want to co-operate with the church, and they can do that best by uniting with it. The fact is they can send their children to church school only up to a certain age. After that the children follow the example of their parents.

In juvenile court a mother complained when her daughter was sentenced to the reform school: "But judge, I always sent her to Sunday school. I thought Sunday school would teach her not to do those things." The judge replied, "Did you say you *sent* her! That meant she understood you didn't believe in it enough to go yourself."

Point out to them: "Your children look skeptically upon an organization you refuse to join. Unite with the church and take your children with you to church and church school."

5. *What a father does appeals to his children.* A boy loves his mother, but he follows his dad.

One evening a visitor returning reported to the pastor: "You remember what you said last night, 'A boy loves his mother, but he follows his dad.' The first home we entered the boy attended our Sunday school, but the father wasn't even a church member. The mother was willing to join, but he wasn't. I talked to him but held back on that idea. I didn't want to tell him with the boy sitting there, but finally nothing else touched him. Then I let him have it. I said, 'You know, a boy loves his mother, but he follows his dad.' He looked like a bombshell had hit his mind. After a stunned moment he turned to his son and said, 'Son, suppose we join the church together!' And, pastor, we secured four members in that family, all on profession of faith."

6. *These are times of stress and strain.* Young people face temptations unheard of in past generations. The future is dark if not hopeless unless people have the stability of a great ship in the storm. Only people with character and religious training can hold out and hold on. The church develops the kind of character parents want in their children. It gives them the kind of Christian manhood and womanhood needed to serve the future. Only a nation with moral stamina and godly powers can endure. The partnership of parents and young people with Christ in the church is their hope.

Select the appropriate talking points

Do not try to use all the talking points at once. Select one or two and adhere to them. Choose the one that appeals most to you and seems most appropriate to the family. Weave it into your conversation.

These and similar reasons are almost invincible to parents who wish the best for their children. True parents will give up almost anything and make almost any sacrifice when seriously confronted with the responsibilities of Christian living for the sake of their children.

Interviewing the children

When you enter a home where there are children, make your approach through them.

First, call the family together. It is much easier to win the parents in the presence of the children than without them. Do not feel embarrassed in discussing their Christian relationships, because the children know the home situation. This is not to take advantage of the parents or to make them lose prestige in the eyes of their children. The welfare of the home must be paramount. In these homes are the future teachers, artists, statesmen, ministers, and peacemakers of the world. God will give you the divine supplement that will help to establish these families on the road to well-being and harmony.

While we are primarily securing youth and adult decisions in this enterprise and are expecting the decisions of the children to come through the church-school teachers, nevertheless we should not pass any opportunity of winning the parents through the children and the children themselves to Christian discipleship along with their parents.

Winning youth to Christ

There are three principles to follow in winning young people to Christ:

First, gain the confidence of youth. Establish a point of contact. Get his good will. Inquire about his interests, his grade in school, whether he belongs to the Boy or Girl Scouts, his class in the church school, his teacher's name, his interest in sports. After he has become at ease with you, you can proceed further.

Second, expect youth to want to be Christian. Jesus always expected the best of people, and they usually responded. We do an injustice to youth when we suppose they operate from wrong motives, and presume that their habits are bad and need to be changed to good ones. Most of these children and youth are already far on the right road. Many of them already love Jesus and are trying to follow in his way. You want them to come all the way, to measure up to the highest, to enlist in Jesus' great cause, to let Christ control all their lives.

Finally, make an appeal to the highest loyalty. Appeal to them to give all in the cause of Christian service. Youth are adventurous, daring, fearless, and they want something to which to dedicate their lives. King Arthur bound his knights

> by so straight vows to his own self,
> That when they rose, knighted from kneeling, some
> Were pale as at the passing of a ghost,
> Some flush'd, and others dazed, as one who wakes
> Half-blinded at the coming of a light.

Jesus wants complete self-commitment, the adventure of a full life. Youth everywhere about the world are giving their young lives, millions of them to wrong causes and to wrong endeavors. Here is the highest cause in all the world. The hope of tomorrow lies in the Christian way of life. Here is the greatest Leader of all the ages. Here is the greatest claim: loyalty to Jesus Christ. Young people will respond to that!

A progressive appeal

Make a progressive appeal. Start with the person in the family who shows the most interest. Usually it will be an older child or a young person. Lead that one step by step from one decision to another until he has made the final commitment to Christ and is ready to unite with the church.

Let the parents listen while you discuss with the children and young people their relationship to Christ. When you get a decision from one of them, if you can pray audibly, ask that they bow their heads together while you thank the heavenly Father. Then secure the decision of the parents. The basis of appeal will be companionship of the family in the Christian life, parents with their children. Excuses pale in the light of parental responsibility to their children. "A little child shall lead them." When the child has made a decision, it is difficult for a parent to refrain. In fact, parents will desire to participate with their children in the Christian life. Usually you will find a ready eagerness to co-operate. Persuasion is not difficult. And you will find the scripture fulfilled. "This day is salvation come to this house."

Family religion

When the members of the family have made their commitments, the visitors should take a few minutes to instruct them. Tell them of the pastor's class in church membership for the children. Then give them some helpful suggestions about religion in the home. Suggest grace before meals, family prayers as well as private prayers, perhaps some family devotional booklet. Emphasize the family habit of regular attendance at the church services where every member of that home shall be present in the congregational worship of God. The importance of this united worship of God should be strongly asserted.

Conclude the visit with a consecration to God. Thank the heavenly Father for the commitments made. Ask his guidance of each one in the family by name. Ask his help in directing their lives in true Christian fidelity and service that his Kingdom may come and his will may be done. The Lord's Prayer joined in by all would be a most appropriate benediction on such a blessed occasion.

With joy in your hearts go to the next home—and remember, return for a final report at nine thirty.

(Conclude this final instruction period with a prayer of dedication for the workers in their sacred endeavor.)

THE GREAT COMMISSION

The first command in the Great Commission of Jesus is not to go to the ends of the earth. It is to be witnesses in Jerusalem. Those who truly testify to the redeeming power of Christ in their home communities inevitably become the most definitely committed to world redemption

This imperative of evangelism is not for individuals alone, but for the abundant life in our age. As beneficent rain is composed of innumerable single drops, so also social movements for the Kingdom of God are composed of Christian individuals. Our service to spread the good news is the only way in which we can honestly pray, "Thy kingdom come, thy will be done." As each person is won, he becomes an integral part of economic justice, racial understanding, and world peace. Finally the knowledge of God can cover the earth as the waters cover the sea.

Here is the gigantic challenge not merely to add names to a church roll but to add Kingdom builders to the hosts of the Lord. As the laymen witness for Christ and their faith, they make possible the extension of the gospel by personal contagion and social action. This redemptive movement of lay evangelism may mean the difference of turning the events of our century to Christ and Christian solutions.

What these trained evangelists do in a single community is beyond imagination. It is impossible to perceive the far-reaching influence of one man or woman, a single boy or girl, won to Christ. Only eternity can give the answer. The outreach of these trained people will never be known until that day at the end of time when all lives shall be as an open book. Then shall the influence of each be visible. Under the Providence of God, there shall be gathered together all those who have been saved. It is probable that then the sum total of it all shall be beyond the comprehension of finite mind.

To us, his followers upon the earth, the challenge for an evangelical revival rings out:

> Whenever there is silence around me
> By day or by night—
> I am startled by a cry.
> It came down from the cross—
> The first time I heard it.
> I went out and searched—
> And found a man in the throes of crucifixion,
> And I said, "I will take you down,"

A WORKABLE PLAN OF EVANGELISM

And I tried to take the nails out of his feet.
But he said, "Let them be,
For I cannot be taken down
Until every man, every woman, and every child
Come together to take me down."
And I said, "But I cannot hear you cry.
What can I do?"
And he said, "Go about the world—
Tell everyone that you meet—
There is a man on the cross."
—Elizabeth Cheney

So we as laymen and ministers shall go about our communities and the world telling everyone that we meet, "There is a Man on the Cross" who can save them, and us, and our world.

"We, according to his promise, look for new heavens and a new earth, wherein dwelleth righteousness." (II Pet. 3:13.)

―――――APPENDIX―――――

An Outline for a Visitation Program
For a Single Church

(Write in the dates and keep up to schedule.)

I. Decide upon the dates of the campaign.
   Dates ...

II. Secure the prospects, by—
   1. Community survey, two months prior to campaign, in co-operation with other churches;
      Date ...
      or—
   2. Community survey, two months prior to campaign, with your church by itself.
      Date ...
   3. Church school survey, beginning two months prior to campaign, lasting four Sundays.
      Date, Sunday. ...
   4. A church Roll Call.
      Date, Sunday. ...
   5. Church register.
   6. Ask members to hand in names.
      Dates ...
   7. The Pastor's notebook.
   8. A check of the church membership register by the pastor and someone else.
      Dates ...
   9. The census sheet or "Welcome Wagon."
      (Begin making up the Prospect and Assignment Cards immediately. Keep constantly up to date until the campaign begins.)

A WORKABLE PLAN OF EVANGELISM

III. Secure the visitors (the pastor's responsibility, his alone) by—
   1. Listing the church members to be prospective visitors during the second month prior to the campaign.
      The month of . . .
   2. Interviewing prospective visitors one month prior to campaign.
      The month of . . .
   3. Securing the consent of the visitors not later than the second week prior to the campaign.
      Deadline date . . .

IV. Set the campaign dates.
   1. First instruction, "Securing the Decision."
      Date . . .
   2. Second instruction, "Efficient Visiting"
      Date . . .
   3. Third instruction, "Difficult Cases"
      Date . . .
   4. Fourth instruction, "Family Visiting,"
      Date . . .

V. Master the instruction talks. (The pastor should spend at least a month familiarizing himself with the four instruction talks.)
   The month of . . .

VI. Decide upon the continuation program, special periods, monthly meetings, etc.
   Dates . . .

DATE DUE